#NoBanNoWall

ELANA MANN, *POSTER FOR TAKE A STAND MARCHING BAND,* 2017, 16 X 20 INCHES, INK JET PRINT

LOS ANGELES REVIEW OF BOOKS

QUARTERLY JOURNAL // NO. 15 // REVOLUTION

COVER ART
JEMIMA WYMAN FRONT: *PINK BLOC PROTESTOR AT GAY PRIDE IN COPACABANA, 13TH OCTOBER 2013*, 2015, DIGITAL IMAGE, SIZE VARIABLE
BACK: *TWO DEMONSTRATORS AT "OPERATION SEA ARRRGH" AGAINST THE CHURCH OF SCIENTOLOGY IN WASHINGTON, DC, 14TH JUNE 2008*, 2015, DIGITAL IMAGE, SIZE VARIABLE

The Los Angeles Review of Books is a 501(c)(3) nonprofit organization. The *LARB Quarterly Journal* is published quarterly by the Los Angeles Review of Books, 6671 Sunset Blvd., Suite 1521, Los Angeles, CA 90028. Submissions for the *Journal* can be emailed to EDITORIAL@LAREVIEWOFBOOKS.ORG. Visit our website at WWW.LAREVIEWOFBOOKS.ORG.

The *LARB Quarterly Journal* is a premium of the LARB Membership Program. Annual subscriptions are available. Go to WWW.LAREVIEWOFBOOKS.ORG/MEMBERSHIP for more information or email MEMBERSHIP@LAREVIEWOFBOOKS.ORG.

Distribution through Publishers Group West. If you are a retailer and would like to order the *LARB Quarterly Journal*, call 800-788-3123 or email orderentry@perseusbooks.com.

To place an ad in the *LARB Quarterly Journal*, email ADSALES@LAREVIEWOFBOOKS.ORG.

CONTENTS

QUARTERLY JOURNAL // NO. 15 // REVOLUTION

ESSAYS

FICTION

POETRY

SHORTS

Dear Reader,

Perhaps we are in a revolution and perhaps we are not. It is sometimes hard to tell. Of course, that can't always be the case, especially in revolutions that are full of violence or bloodshed, but there must be revolutions that we don't see or don't notice or don't totally acknowledge. Or on the flip side, there are events that we are too quick to call by that name, when actually they aren't really anything at all, except steps in a long and drawn out series of accidents.

You will find in this issue of the *LA Review of Books Quarterly Journal*, writers who define revolution in many different ways. In some cases, the revolution is banal — it is people walking back and forth in an office building; the unchanging nature of bureaucracy stays as strong as ever. In others, it is a matter of violence, death, and a forcible redefinition of the self. In others, it is hopeful, long overdue, a sign of better things to come, and a reassuring move in the teleological progress of the world. I find this diversity of definition heartening in itself. What are we if not adaptive creatures? Thank god we don't get sick from the interminable spinning of the world. In fact, we depend on it. Revolution should not be the part that is frightening or unfamiliar; it should be all we know. We should be afraid instead of stagnation and stillness. Standing water festers. You wouldn't drink it, why let it cover your face and your head, and why let yourself sink?

Yours,
Medaya
Editor in Chief, Quarterly Journal

DANIELLE DEAN, *I'M NOT GOING TO ACCEPT NOTHING*, 2017, DIGITALLY PRINTED BANNER, LAMINATED BUSINESS CARD, COLOR PHOTO PRINT, SHOE FLYER, VELVET, WALNUT FRAME, 49 ½ X 52 ½ INCHES / COURTESY THE ARTIST AND COMMONWEALTH AND COUNCIL, PHOTO: RUBEN DIAZ

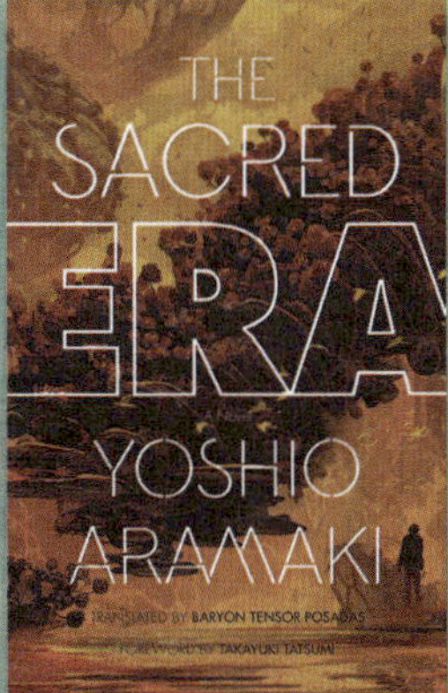

OUT OF
THE BLUE
NEW SHORT
FICTION FROM
ICELAND
HELEN
MITSIOS,
EDITOR
FOREWORD
BY SJÓN

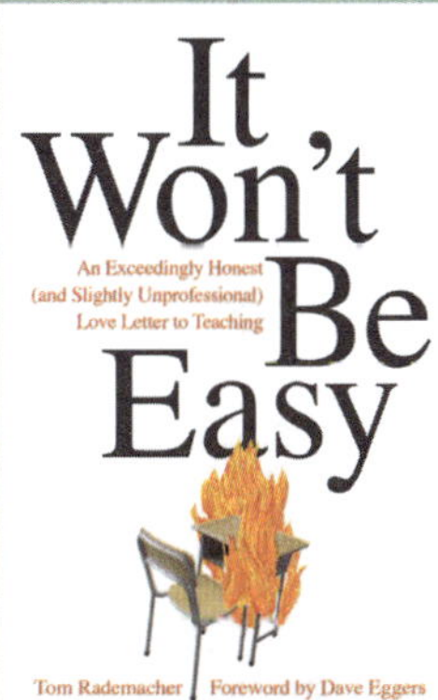

SUMMER READS

FIRST THOUGHT

Conversations with Allen Ginsberg

Michael Schumacher

"Destined to be a perfect companion to any study of Ginsberg, the poet." **—Bill Morgan**, author of *The Typewriter is Holy: The Complete, Uncensored History of the Beat Generation*

$19.95 PAPERBACK | 280 PAGES

THE SACRED ERA

A Novel

Yoshio Aramaki
Translated by Baryon Tensor Posadas
Foreword by Takayuki Tatsumi

"Engrossing in both its imagery and philosophical exploration, *The Sacred Era* traverses the far reaches of the cosmos but ultimately revels in the personal and the human."
—Foreword Reviews

$22.95 PAPERBACK | 272 PAGES

OUT OF THE BLUE

New Short Fiction from Iceland

Helen Mitsios, editor
Foreword by Sjón

"*Out of the Blue* reads like a series of lively dreams, by turns magical and stoic and strange, and each sensational." **—Peter Geye**, author of *Wintering*

$24.95 HARDCOVER | 208 PAGES

IT WON'T BE EASY

An Exceedingly Honest (and Slightly Unprofessional) Love Letter to Teaching

Tom Rademacher

"Rademacher does not hold back . . . his honest, inspiring, and often humorous book will appeal to teachers, future teachers, and those interested in education." ***—Booklist***

$17.95 PAPERBACK | 208 PAGES

University of Minnesota Press
To order call 800-621-2736 • *www.upress.umn.edu*

GLENDA WYMAN AND JEMIMA WYMAN,
PROPAGANDA PATCHWORK, 2016, TEXTILE,
81 X 81 INCHES, (IRREGULAR)

JEMIMA WYMAN, *DEMONSTRATOR AT AN EMERGENCY PROTEST OPPOSING BRADLEY MANNING'S SENTENCING IN WASHINGTON, DC, 21ST AUGUST 2013*, 2015, DIGITAL IMAGE, SIZE VARIABLE

JEMIMA WYMAN, *PROTESTERS AGAINST ISRAELI OCCUPATION, WEST BANK, 10TH OCTOBER 2015 (GREEN AND WHITE STRIPED), BLACK BLOC GROUP DEFENDING ANTI-MORSI PROTESTERS, EGYPT, 11TH FEBRUARY 2013 (RED FACE ON MASK), PROTESTERS OCCUPYING CITY HALL AGAINST THE POLICE SHOOTING OF MICHAEL BROWN PUT A KEFFIYEH ON THE GEORGE WASHINGTON STATUE, CHICAGO, 11TH AUGUST 2012 (STATUE) (STATUE), PROTESTER AGAINST PALESTINIAN DEATHS IN SYRIAN REFUGEE CAMP, PALESTINE, 4TH JANUARY 2014 (GUY FAWKES), ANTI-CAPITALIST DEMONSTRATION, MONTRÉAL, 1ST MAY 2012 (BEIGE HOODIE), PROTESTERS REVOLT AGAINST LABOR AND FISCAL REFORM, MADRID, 31ST MARCH 2012 (ARM BENT), ACTIVIST AGAINST CHEMICAL WEAPONS USED BY FORCES LOYAL TO BASHAR AL-ASSAD, SYRIA, 22ND AUGUST 2013 (GAS MASK), ANTI-GOVERNMENT PROTESTER, MILAN, 14TH DECEMBER 2010 (SCREAMING SKULL), PALESTINIAN PROTESTERS CLASHING WITH ISRAELI TROOPS IN GAZA CITY, 10TH OCTOBER 2015 (PEACE SIGN WITH GLOVE), SUPPORTER OF THE SYRIAN UPRISING RECORDING FELLOW PROTESTERS, BEIRUT, 15TH AUGUST 2011 (MUSTACHE), PARTICIPANT IN MOORS & CHRISTIANS FESTIVAL, SPAIN, 26TH JULY 2009 (SIDE PROFILE), ANTI-ISRAEL AND ANTI-WAR IN GAZA PROTESTER, TORONTO, 10TH JANUARY 2009 (EYES LOOKING LEFT), LABOR DAY PROTESTER, LEBANON, 1ST MAY 2013 (FIST RAISED)*, 2016, HAND-CUT DIGITAL PHOTOGRAPHS, 24 X 14 INCHES (FRAMED)

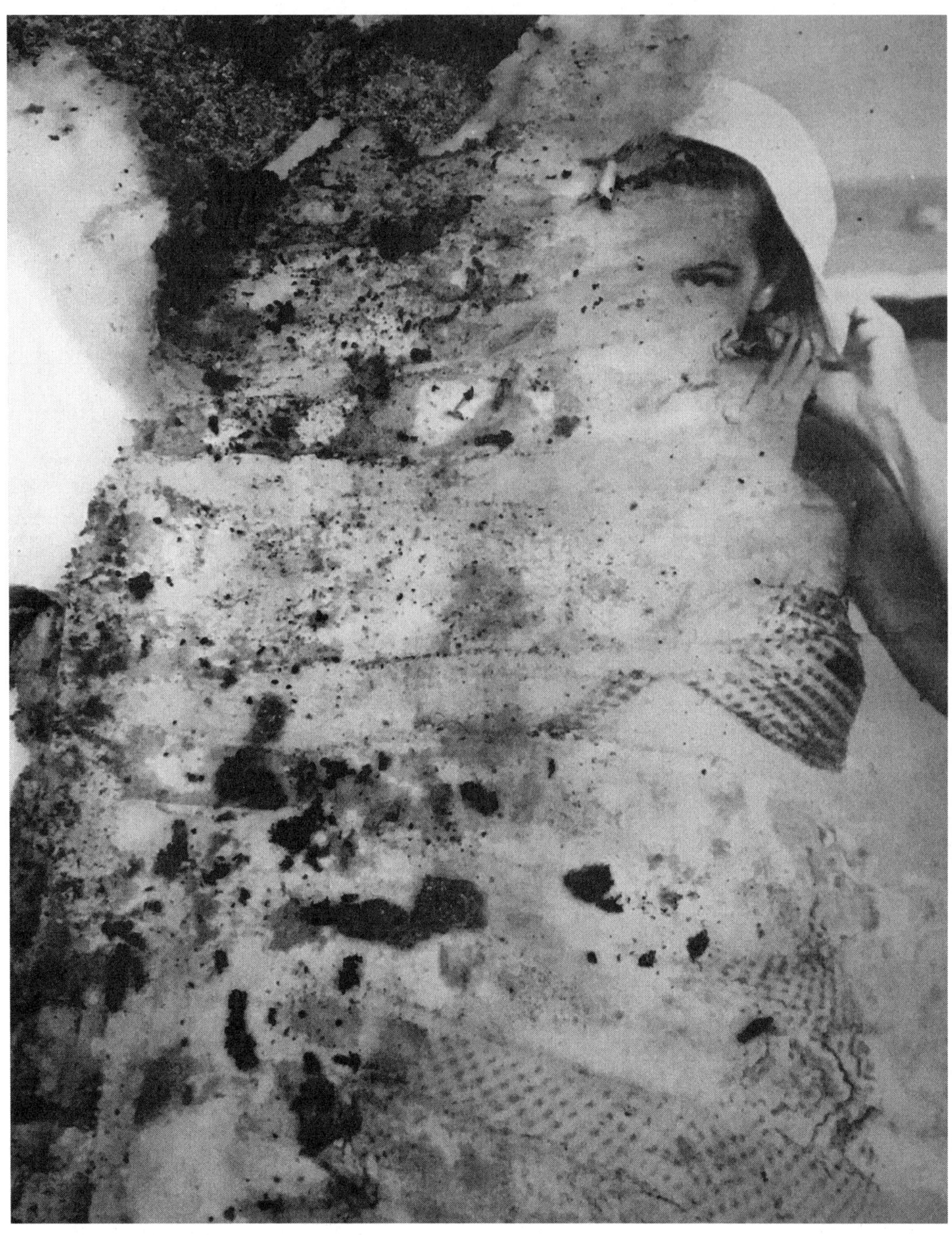

COURTESY OF COLIN DAYAN

HOW TO REMEMBER MY MOTHER

COLIN DAYAN

I SAW SOMETHING on my left cheek. I thought it was a scab. I pulled it off. It was a tick. Less than a 10th of an inch and very light in color, it was a taupe little thing, not big and black like the tick I found on my back just a month ago. I live in Nashville much the way my mother lived in Atlanta, but without her beauty or luxury. As a child, I was in awe of the woman who laughed or screamed at me. She shunned me, but now, dead, she stays close. Sometimes she comes down the wall like a spider.

For years I've been writing her story. I tried in vain to forget her, but she stays around as close to me as my breath. No death counts if the feeling is strong enough.

After she died, boxes arrived from Atlanta. They filled the garage. I gave away her clothes: furs, gowns, sequined sashes, golf shoes, and hats. But I kept my father's photos of her. There were thousands. One had been corroded by water. This photo of my mother just after her marriage shades from pale lilac to ochre to yellow to cobalt blue to gray, as if cinders were eating away at the remnants of color. Her lineaments curve gently in and out of the mold. What shows is one eye, an immaculately plucked brow, a bit of hair covered with something like a hat but more like a towel, pulled down with her hands caught mid-movement. The rest of the body is a blur of fabric dissolved into the waste of wet and dust.

Looking through other photos of my mother, I am not sure how to tell who she was or where she came from. Everything seems make-believe. She told me she was from Paris. Years later, in a taxi going to a restaurant in New York, she began speaking Creole to the driver. She smiled and told me she was Haitian. In trying to tell her story and account for my discomfiture in the world of humans, words like mimicry and falsity come to mind.

I always felt that I was not right in my skin. Everything had to do with race. What mattered most was the quality of hair, the color of skin. She called me "Ubangi." I did not look like her friends' daughters. She did not like me to touch her.

But who was she? As I write this, I remember how she hated to be referred to as "she" or "her." "I have a name," she would say. But even that was a changeable thing. Her real name was Sophie. She never uttered it, changing it occasionally to "Sophia," but most often going by the name her friends gave her when she arrived in Atlanta, still speaking French. They called her "Frenchie." Like her appearance, her name was mutable, adapted to whatever role was demanded, no matter how fantastic.

Appearance was everything. I tried in vain to tell the difference between fantasy and reality.

My mother left Haiti two years after the American occupation ended, moving with her family to Brooklyn, where she met my father and soon married him. When the US Marines finally departed in 1934, Haitians sang words in praise of President Sténio Vincent that my mother later sang to me — but only after my father died. "If there's anyone who loves the people, it's President Vincent," and she sang it to me in Creole: "*Papa Vincent, mesi. Si gen youn moun ki renmen pèp la, se President Vincent.*" In a deep and rapturous voice, she gave thanks for all he, "a mulatto" as he was called at the time, did for the blacks of Haiti, while ruthlessly punishing light-skinned elites. With this one song, she let me in on her secret: she harbored a confounding infidelity to her class and color.

This light-skinned woman, daughter of a Syrian merchant, belted out a couple of lines of the popular merengue recorded by Alan Lomax, who heard it at the elite Club Toland in Port-au-Prince on Christmas Eve, 1936: "This is a guy who loves the people / This is the guy who gives us the right to sell in the streets / He gives us that because he kicked out the Syrians / So we're crying out, thank you Papa Vincent." The self-proclaimed "Second Liberator" allowed the masses to sell goods wherever they could, and curbed the Syrian takeover of retail, shuttering their stores and driving them out.

That same year, my mother traveled from Brooklyn to a honeymoon in Mexico, where she and my father traveled around for two years, then to Nashville, and, finally, to Atlanta. The South must have seemed to her like a cross between Haiti and New York. "I would have been an actress," she told me. "Then I met your father." But she never stopped acting. She lived to be looked at.

After leaving Haiti at the age of 13, my mother never knew beauty or hope again. Everything that followed her departure and her marriage at 17 to a 37-year-old husband seemed useless or dead. When she moved with my father to the Jim Crow South, she exchanged her complex racial origins for the empty costume of white-washed glamour. I didn't realize until now, as I write, just how deluded she was about her real attachments, and just how casually — without really ever knowing the loss — she surrendered her origins to a mask of whiteness.

But in moments of privacy, when not seen by the eyes of others, she used to say things that sounded like incantations. "*Arab manje koulèv*," which in Creole means "Arabs eat snakes." She was never clear about her family or her childhood, explaining that her father told her not to worry about his origins. "It's no good to be too strange in a country you love," he sighed. They never meant anything to me at the time, those words said in the dark of my bedroom.

Years later, I learned they were pieces of the life she had left behind, not just rapt conjuring. Besides "*Mesi, Papa Vincent,*" she repeated, "*Desalin pas vle oue blanc,*" which means "Dessalines doesn't like whites." Late at night when she came into my room, she returned to the beauty and force of her life in Haiti.

Her longing was consecrated most often in this homage to Jean-Jacques Dessalines, who proclaimed Haitian independence in 1804. She praised only the fierce Dessalines — called "barbaric" by most historians — not the urbane Toussaint l'Ouverture or Henri Christophe, who was turned into a god or spirit by the Haitian people. He is still invoked as a *lwa* in vodou ceremonies in the countryside. Rejecting things French and unconcerned about social graces, he fought to give land to ex-slaves who had only recently been considered property themselves.

In the South, my mother concealed her past, even as she remained estranged from the whites around her. By the time my mother got to Nashville, she recognized the necessity of becoming as white as possible. A gilded white lady of the South, that's what my father wanted. Confined by the role she assumed, she performed her new identity. Hiding herself beneath a false smile and pale skin, she wrapped her discomfort and later her sorrow in silks and jewels. This denial of her history was not anything like a grab for white power and privilege, but rather a casual act performed in exchange for a lifestyle of luxury. This false if stylish veneer killed her spirit and destroyed any chance for happiness.

I can reckon with her life and mine only through how far I fell away from whiteness or how close I could come to black. "Who knows what evil lurks in the heart of men? The shadow knows." We lived, my mother and I, in a world that flickered back and forth between black and white, darkness and light. Nothing could be secure.

One day she pulled a magnolia off the tree in our front yard. She grabbed it in her hand like a castanet, shook it, and pulled off the white leaves. "There," she sighed, "There — look — and see the red and the rot." I was astonished by the violence of that gesture and the softness of her voice. She was entranced by whatever had died and gone bad. She knew that it had once lived in beauty.

¤

A white spider too small for me to truly make out its legs came swinging down lightly. It hovered over the pages about my mother, then two filaments came through the sunlight, now onto the desk, then around my cup of tea, then onto other pages, and now it comes toward me. So fragile and precarious that I'm afraid to move: I feel that it enveloped me in its threads. Wrung out from the innards of her being, they loop me into her life.

My mother's past comes to me in flashes: fragments of Sinatra's voice, the sound of laughter or the feel of her slap across my face. Her photos lead me like patches of light into a world that was but is no more. Not long after I brought them into the house, I smashed my nose against the jamb of a doorway, crushed my fingers in a broken garage door, and shattered my ribs in a fall down the stairs. We found each other again when I least expected it; and in sight of her, with her breath on my neck, I know now that whatever mattered to me, the poems I cherished, the writers I taught, and the words I wrote were inspired by her life and raised up again more fiercely after her death.

¤

When she awakened in bed that morning in Mexico City, she looked up at my father in what seemed to be sheer wonderment, or was it just languor in the soft light of a room sometime in midsummer at the beginning of their honeymoon. I had never seen any of these photos, all carefully numbered on their backs in pencil, and kept in two wooden boxes. Only now, with her death behind me, am I struck by expressions that I never saw in life, looks that astonish me in their gentle repose.

Doom is never foretold. Not when you're young, just married to a man who adores you and takes you away to a place of sun, with dust, lizards everywhere in the cracks, birds wandering lost in streets that remind you of Port-au-Prince. She heard the familiar sounds of suffering and holiness in the bodies of beggars and priests. How bad could things be if you had a gold bracelet on your wrist given to you by a doting husband? She especially liked to see the statues of the Virgin that appeared miraculously on the steps of churches or on altars with candles, gold chalices, violets, and white carnations.

In 1939, right after their marriage, my parents arrived in Mexico. My father drove his Buick Roadmaster convertible from Guadalajara to Cuernavaca, stopping in Mexico City, traveling along roads Graham Greene first captured with his "whisky priest" in *The Lawless Roads* and then a year later in *The Power and the Glory*, but I doubt they ever read him. My father didn't like Catholics. I do not know any details of their journey. No one ever told me stories. All that remains of the visit are photographs. They got there seven years after Hart Crane leapt off the *Orizaba* into the sea; eight years after Sergei Eisenstein began the film that would be cut and mangled in Hollywood; a year after Malcolm Lowry was deported, his life with the alluring Jan Gabrial a shambles.

My parents began their marriage when the New York World's Fair opened with the debut of nylon stockings, when Billie Holiday first sang and recorded "Strange Fruit," Judy Garland sang "Somewhere Over the Rainbow" in *The Wizard of Oz*, and *Gone with the Wind* premiered at Loew's Grand Theater in Atlanta. Franco had just conquered Madrid, ending the Spanish Civil War. They arrived in Mexico a year before Trotsky was axed to death, at a time when over 1,000 American tourists a month visited Mexico, and artists too. None of this — no history, culture, or politics — can be gleaned from these photographs.

The suffering of bulls, yes, and the remarkable poses of my mother, but besides a few scenes of peasants, cacti, churches, murals, or horses, there was only a 17-year-old girl, chosen by a man 20 years older, continuously reinvented in split-second exposures, caught in hundreds of ways: lying down in a two-piece bathing suit on rocks, or sitting, long legs crossed doubly graceful in the rise of the stairs underneath her, or sometimes standing in sunlight, her head rocked to the side and eyes like tinder.

COURTESY OF COLIN DAYAN

The bulls mattered to her life, even if she didn't know it then or ever. My father went to bullfights. During those afternoons, what did my mother do? As I remember her broken life, I can't stop thinking about the bulls, isolated from their kind, released into spectacle, performing their agony. Three quarters of a century later, I look at the pictures. Out of boxes and other wooden and steel containers, and buried deep under other albums, come these relics of a honeymoon. They were not part of anything I knew, nor did they make up any kind of beauty my parents might retrieve about a past when they might have known love or passion.

I thought these photos might tell me something about their past that would otherwise be lost forever. My mother's face, caught in poses that were never off-guard or random, still does not speak to me. Sometimes she has that immaculate quality of being purified of anything living. When she looks out at my father, the hand drawn up on one side, sultry on the hip, I think of Rita Hayworth, her idol. The earliest films of this love goddess were on my mother's mind when she left for Mexico with my father.

What more can be known about the honeymoon that left my mother cold, my father clueless? I'm sure that my mother never looked at any of these photos. She had no interest in remembering the past. Her indifference to what she had felt then made her the woman that I grew up knowing. I admired and feared her, but most of all I longed to be close to her, enveloped in the waves of her brown and heavy hair. Just a couple of years after marriage, the soft face of a woman beguiled became impenetrable in its exacting beauty. A veneer set in over her luscious skin, hardness seemed to take over eyes that were once inviting, her smile frozen for the camera. But that unyielding stiffness had not yet set her face in stone. She was not afraid to be vulnerable, and her eyes looked at what she thought she loved.

¤

"Blood poured down the streets," my mother used to repeat after my father died. Cryptic, she never explained who or what she meant. She liked to hear church bells ringing. She prayed the words she learned as a child in Port-au-Prince, where the nuns at Sacré Coeur, her school in Turgeau, took away the girls' mirrors and then gazed secretly at themselves: "*Je vous salue Marie, pleine de grâce, le seigneur est avec vous.*" When she worshipped the Virgin late in life, she told me how God once loved a woman pure and without stain. Then she got confused, and remembered how hard it was to remain pure, especially when you hear stories about the *djablesse*, or "she-devil." The most feared ghost in Haiti, she is condemned to walk the woods before entering heaven as punishment "for the sin of having died a virgin." She laughed. "Think about all those nuns taught they'd go to heaven, but they end up wandering around looking for what they never got or scaring the hell out of those who have it." With a throaty whisper, she added: "They get you coming and going."

In Mexico her marriage began with prayers to the Virgin of Guadeloupe, our lady of the hills and patroness of the Indians and the poor, so beautiful in a blue mantle, dotted with stars; with the killing of priests, the ice-ax murder of Trotsky, my father's hero; and a ride on a Ferris wheel that she never forgot. Each parent lost something that mattered that year in Mexico: my father, his revolution; my mother, her virginity.

She kept repeating things. Round and round, always circling back to the gold coins she threw in fountains, the stones that hit dogs, or the sun that was always too hot. Sixty years later, she recalled things I'd never heard her mention before. Not in sentences, but fragments, words thrown like skipping stones on water. "The sun burns the dust at my feet." "Two more dogs bled, hit again with stones." "Gold coins, I have a bracelet of coins." Sun. Dust. Dogs. Coins. Because they never talked about their Mexico adventure, I had no idea what she meant when she called out these things at the end of her life. The photos before me bring it all back, her memories made visible.

"You remember how scared you got on our honeymoon," my father said to my mother one day when I was a child, "how you ran from the wheel, and it just kept turning, and you never stopped running." He said nothing more. Only now do I understand that he must have wanted his young bride to go for a ride with him on the wheel that spun in the sky.

In Malcolm Lowry's *Under the Volcano*, set on the Day of the Dead in 1938, Consul Geoffrey Firmin rides with his beloved Yvonne on "the huge looping-the-loop machine" high on the hill in the tremendous heat "in the hub of which, like a great cold eye, burned Polaris, and round and round it here they went [...] they were in a dark wood." That feeling of entrapment in time that circled on itself, ominous in its repetition, the return of a past that will not quit, reminds me of my parents' lives. Perhaps their unhappiness was already fixed in the image of this wheel turning, not just in actuality, but also, and around the same time, in Sergei Eisenstein's unfinished film *¡Qué Viva México!*

All that remained of his visionary epic — mutilated in Hollywood — were three short features that pandered to commercial, and, some argued, fascist interests. Culled from over 200 thousand feet of film rushes, *Thunder Over Mexico*, *Eisenstein in Mexico*, and *Death Day* were released between the autumn of 1933 and early 1934. The last, which Lowry must have seen, features the "Dance of the Heads." The Ferris wheel revolves dead center, while in the foreground are dancers, and hovering there are three death's heads, human skulls, whether real or masks it does not matter: not for this story of dashed hopes, where everything seemed purposely to turn life into death, but a death more vibrant than anything life offered, in a land where stone lured more than flesh.

The dead do not die. My mother knew that the earth was squirming with spirits. At any moment she might be caught off guard. While she tangled with things too luscious to be put to rest, mostly the unseen, my father was busy using his photographic techniques to pin down patterns of light and dark, to capture brave matadors at the kill, people on the street, the campesinos in the countryside, women at market, but, most of all, his wife, transforming her into an artifact, as if her body had been raised up from rock and conceived anew in rolls of film.

COURTESY OF COLIN DAYAN

In one photo he called "Sun Worshipper," my mother stretches, head thrown back in ecstasy, hair a glossy smooth brown, one leg bent. Her body takes up most of the frame. With the mountains dwarfed behind her, she appears so fluid that she seems to recline sitting up. Years later, it won an award at the High Museum in Atlanta. I remember my father's long nights down in the darkroom when my mother had already turned her back on him.

At no time did my father refer to their time in Mexico, though he kept and treasured a heavy wool blanket with many-colored stripes, tightly woven, with the shape of what I remember as the indigo blue, orange, and white lineaments of a face like an Aztec god. The other precious remnants of their time together were an elaborate silver water pitcher, sugar bowl, creamer, and large hand-hammered tray. As long as my parents lived, this baroque display that seemed to me heavy as lead remained in the dining room.

DANIEL GONZÁLEZ, *AUTHORITY OF THE SOVEREIGN*, 2004, @PRINTGONZALEZ, © DANIEL GONZÁLEZ

THE MEXICAN REVOLUTION: TERRITORIALIZATION AND POTENTIALITY

IGNACIO M. SÁNCHEZ PRADO

THERE HAS RECENTLY been an undeniable intensification in revolution as a topic of inquiry. We can ascribe this growing interest to the late-neoliberal catastrophe and the dire need to see future horizons of political action. And yet, this intensification requires reflection: where do our utopian impulses and desires enter into dialectical tension with revolutionary experiences of the past?

As Saskia Sassen describes in her most recent book, *Expulsions: Brutality and Complexity in the Global Economy*, the current hegemony of capitalism, defined as it is by expulsion and brutality, points toward the need of thinking of a revolution to come, but this future should be considered in the context of the many failed revolutionary projects of the 20th century. I think Mexico offers a particularly instructive case for discussing revolution today — it is a country that underwent one of the most important revolutionary experiences of the 20th century; active revolutionary energies flow through the veins of the body politic even today. And yet, the Mexican revolution is rarely given its due. In part this is because Eurocentrism still holds in the American, French, and Russian Revolutions as the essential trinity in the processes of modernity; Cuban Revolution traditionally garners more attention because of its central role in the development of the Cold War. The Mexican Revolution, however, precisely because of its unique features and outcomes, has a lot to teach contemporary thinkers about the revolutionary.

The term "Mexican Revolution" actually refers to a *longue durée* historical process that has its origins in the gradual collapse of the Porfirian regime; it properly begins with the simultaneous explosion of various rebellions and riots in 1910. It has a military period of about a decade, followed by two more decades of institutional consolidation; it eventually evolves into a single-party regime that ruled Mexico until the General Elections in the summer of 2000. On July 2, Vicente Fox was voted into office, unseating the Institutional Revolutionary Party, which at that point, had been in power for nearly a century. It was during those decades that the Mexican Revolution constructed a cultural hegemony that has few if any parallels in the world — a sense of cultural identity and political subjectivity that very much remains part of the country's experience today. This hegemony also spared Mexico from some of the most violent events in 20th-century Latin America.

The PRI (otherwise known as the Institutional Revolutionary Party, the ruling party that emerged from the Revolution) was in many ways a "perfect dictatorship," as Mario Vargas Llosa called it. Once the party came into power, it took on a corporate nation-state structure, along with significant systems of repression and coercion. At the same time however, Mexico was the only major Latin American country to avoid the cycles of coups, military dictatorships, and US imperial interventions that defined the rest of the continent. Of course, there was violence in Mexico during those years — guerrilla movements were brutally suppressed by the state — but these experiences did not even come close to the political violence in Colombia or the radicalization of groups like the Shining Path in Peru. Mexico had its own "Dirty War" but it did not reach the totalitarian levels seen in places like Argentina. As Gilbert Joseph and Jürgen Buchenau explain in their excellent book *Mexico's Once and Future Revolution*, the blend of "social reform, political coercion and incorporation and cultural hegemony" that defined the Mexican revolution provides a fundamental case study for political scientists, historians, and theorists seeking to account for revolutionary experiences.

In those terms, the Mexican Revolution was a true Event: it redefined the horizon of the possible and the thinkable in the country. And even today, even though the structures of concrete governance have faded, the most dissident of movements still think within its terms. This is why the indigenous uprise of the 1990s in Chiapas was named after Zapata, the architect of rural rebellion and reform in the Revolution. It is the reason why Francisco Villa, the bandit that took Mexico's north by storm, still remains a central icon in political organizations of all kinds. It is also why contemporary left-wing politicians, like Andrés Manuel López Obrador, have kept the Revolution's undelivered and incomplete promises (economic sovereignty, land reform, labor organization, popular education) as central elements of their platforms.

One way of thinking about the Mexican Revolution in the current global crucible is through the tension between the symbolic and the concrete that defined it. The key Evental trait of the Mexican Revolution was the consolidation and emergence of a "people" that, even if fleetingly, created spaces of horizontality and multitudinal organization that upended structures of historical and internal colonialism. In *The Mexican Exception*, Gareth Williams discusses how the Aguascalientes Convention of 1914 — when Villa and Zapata tried to form a revolutionary government — offers a glimpse of the interregnum in sovereignty and the construction of a real, if fleeting, horizontality. Post-Independence 19th-century Mexico was defined by a constant state of Civil War between two camps: the *criollo* (European descent) elite, conservatives who imagined a monarchical state with deep ties to Catholicism, and the liberals, who sought a federal republic with a clear separation between church and state, and who, of course, ultimately prevailed. This conflict cost Mexico half of its territory (the divisions were instrumental in allowing the United States to invade Mexico) and caused long-term financial troubles (the French invasion of the 1860s was justified by a credit default). Further, the war did nothing to address the issues of the country's indigenous and peasant majorities, nor the suffering of the gradually emerging industrial proletariat, those who worked in mining and developing industries like the railroad. Old inequalities, themselves rooted in violence and colonialism, only intensified during Porfirio Díaz's regime, which lasted from 1884 to 1911. Even though Díaz managed to pacify the country and involve it in the transnational trends of capitalist modernization, by the end of his last term, class inequalities had only grown worse.

The Mexican Revolution began as an aggregate of uprisings — landmark mining strikes, protests on Díaz's unwillingness to allow free elections, peasant uprisings, and other phenomena — but they were not spontaneous. As scholars like Bruno Bosteels and Carlos Illades have demonstrated, these revolutionaries built on the longstanding idea of the commune as a form of social organization and they protested within the utopian socialist and anarchist traditions, which had deep roots in the 19th century and which influenced key revolutionary leaders like the Flores Magón brothers. And yet, the outcome of these uprisings, did produce something completely new: it was the beginning of the imagination of a Mexican people. As peasant armies marched into Mexico City, as workers organized into larger and more visible unions, and as the emergent urban bourgeoisie challenged the longstanding power of large-scale rural landowners, Mexico began reenvisioning the people who exercised the sovereignty of the State.

Ostensibly, the Mexican Revolution was as much about redistributing the means of production as it was about the demand of a liberal democracy. Zapata's motto was "Land belongs to those who work it" and, during the presidency of Lázaro Cárdenas (1934–1940), the government instituted key reforms like the nationalization of oil, the major redistribution of land, and a fostering of unionization. Because the Mexican Revolution lacked the centralized plan that defined other communist revolutions, the construction of hegemony in Mexico became a more complex ordeal. The state faced numerous hurdles and it ultimately failed in the construction of economic justice — a failure that has proven to be foundational to Mexico's violent situation today — cultural hegemony became an essential factor. As Horacio Legrás discusses in *Culture and Revolution*, Mexican revolutionary culture achieved a very important feat: for the first time, Mexico as such could be experienced as a "totality." The revolution created a consciousness and a sense of history in Mexico that remains crucial to its citizens and its migrants. The mobilization of the arts and the humanities, from popular theater and muralism to national cinema, still serves the revolutionary imagination, along with the construction of a complex set of Ideological State Apparatuses grounded in one of the most large-scale public education reforms in human history. Taken together, this change has created a sense of belonging and unity that, for better or worse, allowed Mexicans to feel Mexican.

There are many problems, of course, with how this played out. Identity became a way to obscure economics. The idea of the "pueblo mexicano" as a unit was central for the PRI to emerge as a hegemonic power, and for Mexico to avoid building a more agonistic democracy in which the revolutionary tensions could continue their dialectical development. This is more or less the consensus of many scholars today: Roger Bartra called the idea of Mexicanness an "imaginary network of political power," following Cornelius Castoriadis's notion of "imaginary institutions of society." Scholars like Beatriz Urías Horcasitas, Claudio Lomnitz-Adler, and Joshua Lund have compellingly studied how the idea of the Mestizo was rendered possible, in part, by eugenic ideas of race and by secret practices of racism. Indeed, as Pedro Ángel Palou contends in a recent book, one could say that the Mestizo project was failed all along, as the synthesis it sought never actually materialized. While this line of critique is salient (I myself have contributed to it), one must also keep in mind that the cultural hegemony of the PRI created forms of political subjectivities and mobilization that remain crucial in the practices of resistance and emancipation today.

Mexico's cultural revolution may have been a project of state formation (a famous collection of scholarly research called revolutionary practices "everyday forms of state formation"), but one of its crucial effects was modes of identity and subjectivity with revolutionary potentials far beyond the reach of traditional discipline. Muralism today, as Bruce Campbell writes in his excellent book, has gone from the grandiloquent state projects of the 20th century to a popular practice used by various communal organizations — from women's groups in impoverished urban sectors to the Zapatistas themselves — to imagine and organize resistance. Traces of the political potentiality of revolutionary culture are also palpable in the organization of the Mexican American and Chicano movement, where murals of icons like the Virgin of Guadalupe, ideas of the Mestizo canon like the "cosmic race," and Aztlán have been deployed for decades to combat anti-Mexican racism and to provide frameworks of subjectivity to various pro-migrant, labor, and other emancipatory movements. The crucial lesson of the Mexican Revolution is the importance of imagining galvanizing forms of subjectivity and *communitas*, whose potentiality is not exhausted by the realpolitik of everyday governing. The formation of that subjectivity is the revolutions main success. Its failure speaks to what still needs to be done: the creation of forms that better embody the economic demands that underlie revolutionary uprise. If the Mexican revolution as an idea and as a set of principles has managed to survive the failure of the political system it engendered, it is because it became not only the political materiality of a nation-state, but also a matrix of political potentialities that the hegemonic regime was never able to fully discipline, territorialize, and co-opt. This, I think, is the fundamental historical lesson that the Mexican revolution has for revolutionary movements to come.

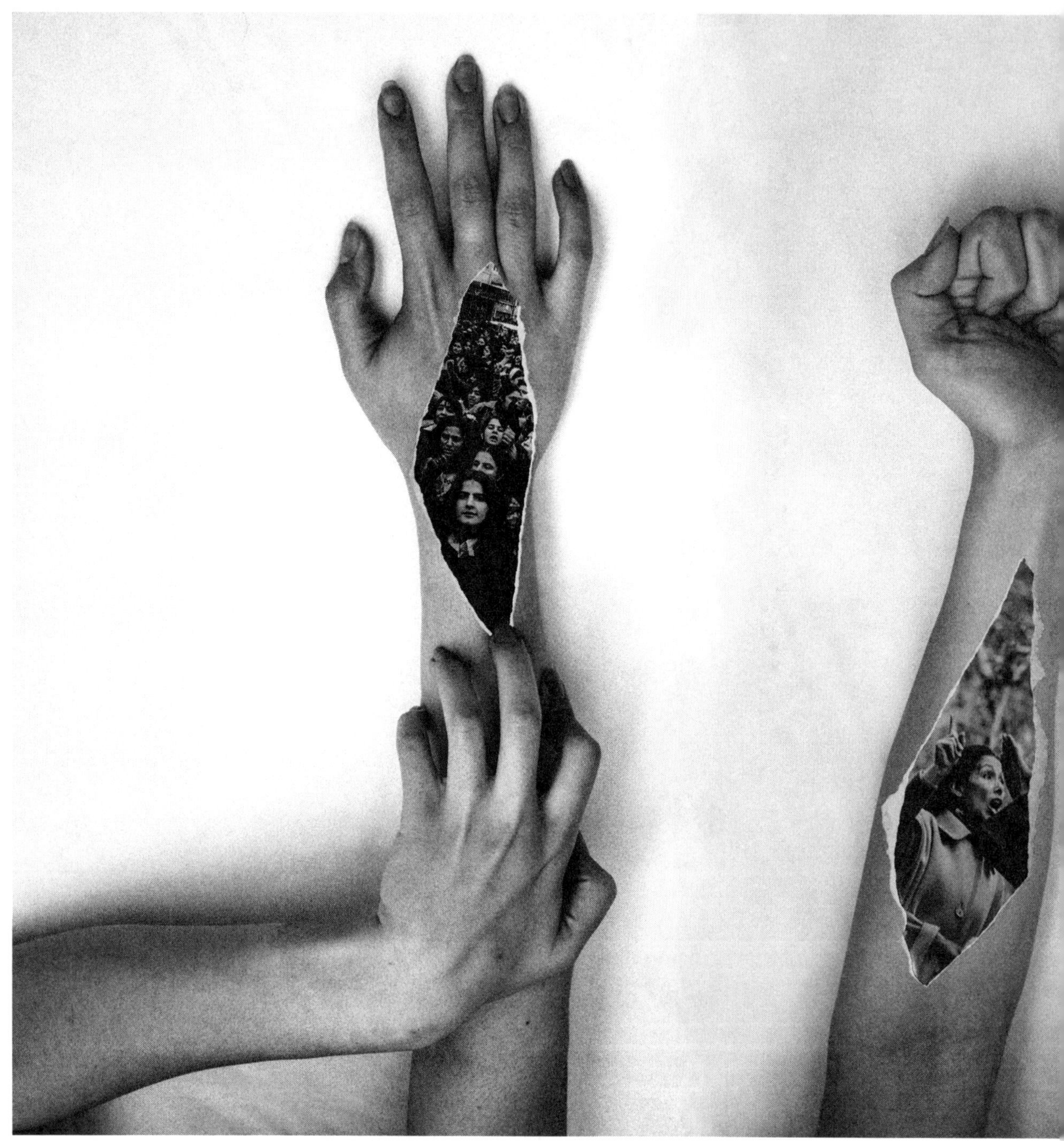

SANAZ KHOSRAVI, *BEYOND MY BLOOD* (FROM THE *REVOLUTION IS NOT OVER* SERIES), 2016

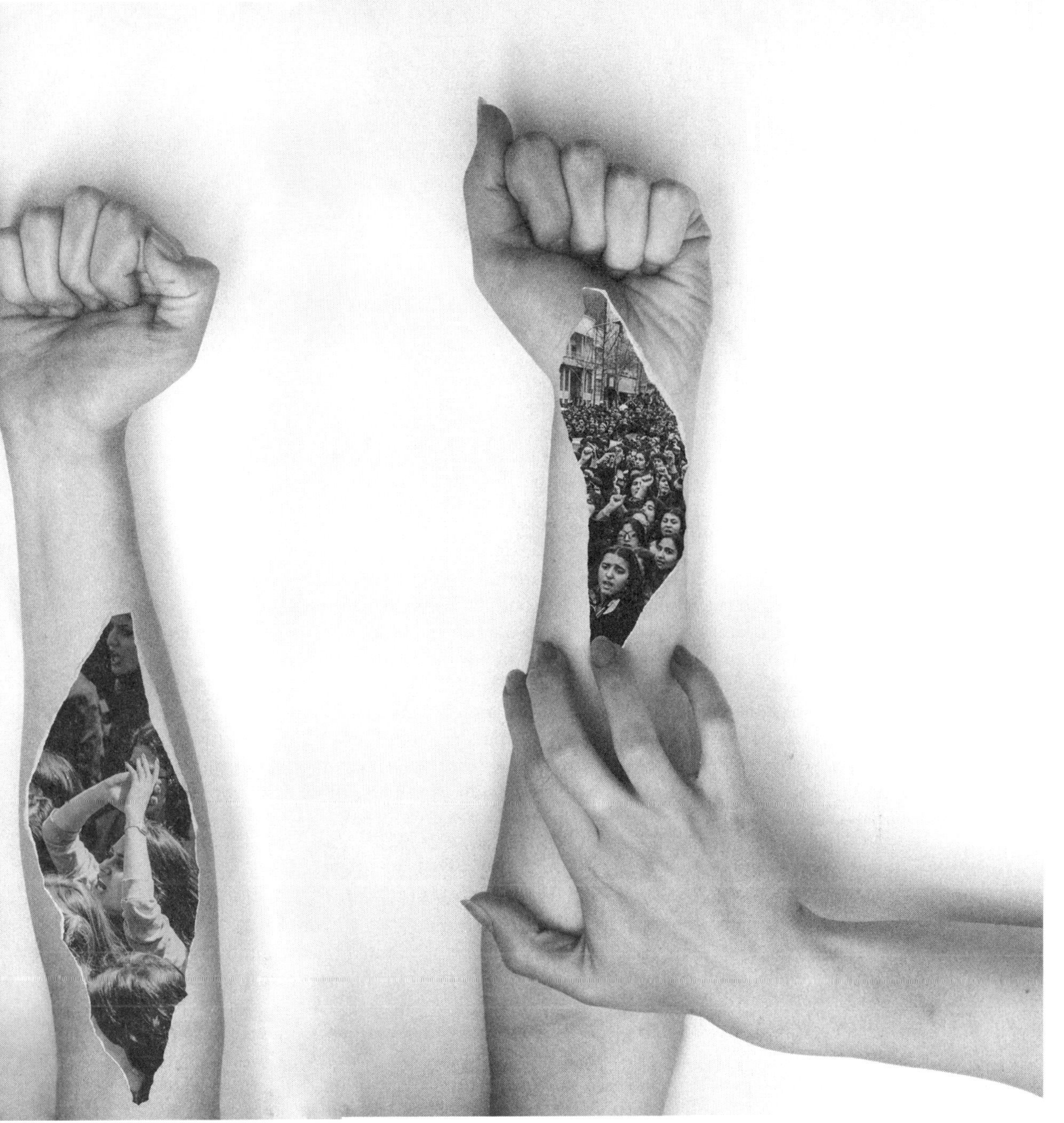

THE REBEL GIRL

EVELYN MCDONNELL

IN 1915, JOE HILL was living in the last home he would ever know: a Salt Lake City prison. But the songwriter, immigrant, and labor activist who had fought for free speech on the streets of Spokane and for socialist revolution in Mexico wasn't about to let jail bars keep him from composing musical bars. Among the tunes he wrote while fruitlessly awaiting appeals on Utah's death row was "The Rebel Girl." The song was an early feminist anthem, a rank-and-file challenge to chauvinistic proletarians as well as a tender ode to an inspirational American muse, the soapbox firebrand Elizabeth Gurley Flynn. In two verses and a chorus, protest song, Hill calls for the global labor movement to perform the radical act of advocating for the work of seamstresses as well as miners, all while celebrating the revolutionary leader renowned for her speeches.

Nearly eight decades later, the punk band Bikini Kill recorded a three-song single with rock 'n' roll legend Joan Jett at the production helm. The record included a song called "Rebel Girl," inspired by the spoken-word artist Juliana Luecking, "a dyke on a trike" who "has the revolution in her hips." It's a celebration of courageous women that is not unlike Hill's paean to Flynn and the other "women of many descriptions in this queer world."

There have been few efforts to connect the dots between these two anthems. Bikini Kill themselves seem to have been initially unaware of the songwriter and woman whose legacy they inhabit. Some have noticed an affinity: in 1996, the band Beezus released a sharply conceived and emotionally executed mash-up of the Hill and Kill tunes. A couple of scholars, fanzine writers, and critics have noted the existence of both songs without pursuing their connection. And yet, there is undoubtedly a relationship there. Over 100 years ago, an immigrant laborer noticed the shared interests of the workers and the women of the world, inspired by a female revolutionary who saw the liberation of the proletarian as central to the progress of the United States. Hill's lost gem was ahead of its time — it made a powerful call for class and gender intersectionalism. Inadvertently, the flagship band of the 1990s feminist-punk revolution chose the same words for the title of their ode to the empowered individual, and inspired a movement. In the move from the pre-modernist Rebel Girl of the suffragette era to the post-modernist Riot Grrrl of Third Wave feminism, a baton was passed — but where is it now?

Joe Hill is a foundational figure in the history of protest music; he is the progenitor for Woody Guthrie, Bob Dylan, Bruce Springsteen, Rage Against the Machine, Bikini Kill. Born Joel Emanuel Hägglund in Sweden on October 7, 1879, he emigrated to the United States with his brother Paul 23 years later, along with thousands of other low-skilled workers drawn by promises of great fortune (of course, the reality was quite different — corporations sought to flood the labor pool and deflate wages). He Americanized his name, first to Joseph Hillstrom, then to Joe Hill. He became involved in the Industrial Workers of the World, a.k.a. the Wobblies, the union and political movement that led some of the most important strikes in the country during the first decades of the 1900s. Hill traveled the country, following both the work and the resistance from San Francisco, to Portland, to Spokane, to San Pedro, and eventually, fatally, to Utah. He lived the typical life of a Wobbly he took itinerant work, rode the rails and frequently found himself in trouble with the law.

Led by such figures as Bill Haywood, the Magón brothers, Eugene V. Debs, Vincent St. John, and Elizabeth Gurley Flynn, the IWW was arguably the most successful mass radical movement in American history. Ardently anticapitalist, they eschewed the ballot box for the soap box, the strike, and even sabotage. Hill was among the American activists who went to Mexico to help the Magóns overthrow the autocracy of Porfirio Díaz in 1911. He was also active in the free speech fights in Spokane and San Diego in 1908 and 1912, when thousands of speakers standing on soap boxes were imprisoned. The latter occasion was a crucial chapter in the history of the First Amendment — so many bindlestiffs and wage slaves turned out to defend their rights to assembly and expression that the police were overwhelmed and gave up.

Alongside the soapbox, one of the primary ways the IWW motivated its members was through the power of song. Songs were written to describe injustices, as well as inspire action and solidarity. The union raised money by selling songbooks. Joe Hill, who had a knack for clever rhymes and powerful images, eventually became the most famous of the Wobbly songwriters. He once wrote this description of his craft from jail:

> A pamphlet, no matter how good, is never read more than once, but a song is learned by heart and repeated over and over; and I maintain that if a person can put a few cold, common sense facts into a song, and dress them [...] up in a cloak of humor to take the dryness off them, he will succeed in reaching a great number of workers who are too unintelligent or too indifferent to read a pamphlet or an editorial in economic science.

Perhaps Hill's most enduring song is "The Preacher and the Slave," his attack on the Salvation Army. The Starvation Army, as Hill dubbed them, were seen as collaborators with the authorities in the free speech fights because their orchestras would drown out protesters on street corners. In the song's famous refrain, Hill mocks the church's promise of a heavenly reward at the expense of earthly justice: "You'll get pie in the sky when you die." Hill also wrote "Casey Jones — the Union Scab," "The White Slave," and "There Is Power in a Union." In "Mr. Block," he satirized the poor grunts who believed capitalists' promises to look out for their interests. Wobs, as the IWW activists were called for short, loved to belt the chorus, urging Mr. Block to "tie on a rock to your block and jump in the lake / Kindly do that for Liberty's sake."

By 1914, the rich and the powerful recognized the IWW as a preeminent threat to their interests, and many sheriffs, mayors, legislators, and governors were looking for ways to shut the organization down. At the end of that year, Joe Hill found himself in Salt Lake City, looking for work. On January 10, a shopkeeper in Salt Lake City was murdered in his store along with his son; another son returned fire and survived. That same night, Hill showed up at the home of a surgeon with a bullet wound. Three days later, the police arrested the songwriter for homicide. The evidence was thin and circumstantial, but Hill was a Wobbly, and the local press helped whip up a firestorm of hate. The accused didn't help his case by refusing to explain how he had gotten his injury, though, as Hill said, in American law, he didn't need to prove his innocence; the court had to prove his guilt. Since then, historians of the case have found convincing evidence that Hill was shot by a friend in jealousy over a shared love interest. At the time, his supporters lauded his integrity for refusing to betray the identity of his friend or romance. Still, Hill was convicted and sentenced to death.

The effort to free Joe Hill quickly became a cause célèbre, taken up by the IWW. Among those who wrote to Joe in jail and came to Salt Lake City to champion his vindication was Elizabeth Gurley Flynn. Flynn — or, as Haywood, Hill, and others liked to call her, Gurley — was another colorful and compelling figure from this critical period for the American left. Raised in New York City, she was the daughter of immigrants who brought their radical political views with them from Ireland. She made her first public speech, entitled "What Socialism Will Do for Women," at age 16, and was arrested for blocking Manhattan streets at the same age. One of the "She-Dogs of Anarchy," as the *Los Angeles Times* called her, she had a fierce oratory style: "She had an odd manner of making what might be called short-hand gestures, pothooks, curves, dots and dashes written in the air," wrote one reporter. In fact, she had such intense physical charisma that producer David Belasco tried to recruit her to star on Broadway shortly after that first arrest. Bursting with girl power, the teenager told him, "I don't want to be an actress! I want to speak my own words and not say over and over again what somebody else has written. I'm in the labor movement and I speak my own piece!" Speak her own piece she did — over and over —helping to rally workers from Minnesota to Lawrence, Massachusetts, to Paterson, New Jersey, to Spokane. Later, she became a founding member of the American Civil Liberties Union and a powerful supporter of Sacco and Vanzetti, the two Italian anarchists, who were convicted of murdering a guard in 1920.

Gurley was the rare female leader of the Wobblies. She often spoke to textile workers and the wives of strikers about the rights of women, though she was by no means ghettoized to such interests and audiences. In her long skirts and with her broad gestures, she inspired the men too. "To the working class she's a precious pearl," Hill wrote in "The Rebel Girl." "She brings courage, pride and joy / To the fighting Rebel Boy." In "The Rebel Girl," Hill also calls out the gendered myopia of the labor movement: "We've had girls before, but we need some more." In fact, he was an admirer of Gurley's and advocate of a more inclusive union even before he met her. In a December 1914 letter to the Wobbly newspaper *Solidarity*, he wrote that women "are more exploited than the men," and that the IWW's neglect of their concerns had "created a kind of one-legged, freakish animal of a union."

Joe and Elizabeth met only once: she visited him in jail in May 1915. He was on death row because of a romance gone awry, while she was involved with the Italian activist Carlo Tresca, but it seems likely that there was a spark between them. "Joe writes songs that sing, that lilt and laugh and sparkle, that kindle the fires of revolt in the most crushed spirit and quicken the desire for fuller life in the most humble slave," she wrote. "He has crystallized the organization's spirit into imperishable form, songs of the people — folk songs."

They spent one hour together, talking; it was the first time he had been allowed to meet someone outside of his cell. She described their meeting:

> We sat in the sheriff's office, looking out the open barred door at the wide expanse of a beautiful lawn. It was spring in the garden city of Salt Lake, encircled by great mountains, crowned with eternal snows. In springtime its green shimmer, high altitude, and clear pure air were like wine.

They mostly talked about Wobbly business. She reported him as tall and good-looking, but "naturally thin after sixteen months in a dark, narrow cell." He was not maudlin about his fate, but he did tell her, "I'm not afraid of death, but I'd like to be in the fight a little longer." As she left, he joked to her about a man outside, cutting the grass: "He's a Mormon, and he's had two wives and I haven't even had one yet."

They exchanged letters regularly. She fought fearlessly for his release, taking his case all the way to the president of the United States. After meeting with Gurley and her friend Edith Cram, Woodrow Wilson wrote a letter asking the governor of Utah to reconsider Hill's death sentence — to no avail. On November 18, 1915, Joe wrote his last letter to Elizabeth, saying "you have been more to me than a Fellow Worker. You have been an inspiration and when I composed The Rebel Girl you was right there and helped me all the time [...] be sure to locate a few more Rebel Girls like yourself, because they are needed and needed badly." To Bill Haywood, he sent a telegram: "Good-by Bill, I will die like a true-blue rebel. Don't waste any time in mourning — organize." Joe Hill was executed the following day by a firing squad.

After the Palmer Raids broke the back of the IWW in the 1920s, Elizabeth Gurley Flynn became a member and eventual leader of the Communist Party. She was imprisoned for more than two years for her political affiliation during the McCarthy era, when she was in her 60s. In 1964, she died in Russia, where she was working on a revision of her autobiography, *The Rebel Girl*.

In 1991, Bikini Kill singer Kathleen Hanna was living in Washington, DC, where she met and befriended Juliana Luecking, whose single "Wheel" had partly inspired Hanna's own interest in spoken-word performance. When they first met, Queen Juliana, as she was known, showed Hanna some videos of her performances and her "crazy spray-painted bike," then they walked around DuPont Circle, winding up at a dance party hosted by the political punk band Nation of Ulysses. A short time later, Kathleen invited Juliana to a Bikini Kill show, where she dedicated a new song to the performance artist with the gently ironic and determinedly unapologetic style.

MANFRED MÜLLER, *GLACIEM FRIGORE* / © MANFRED MÜLLER, COURTESY OF ROSEGALLERY

In many ways "Rebel Girl" is an ode to the queer culture that Queen Juliana embodied and Hanna, who has identified herself as bisexual, admired. "In her kiss, there's revolution," Hanna sang four years before Jill Sobule kissed a girl. (Juliana says their relationship was platonic.) In the version of the song recorded with Joan Jett, Kathleen sings, "They say she's a dyke but I know, she is my best friend." In other versions, dyke becomes "slut" and the song becomes an attack on slut shaming, decades before that became a term. The song shouts out, in its wonderfully prurient adolescent voice, female sovereignty ("that girl thinks she's the queen of the neighborhood, and I have news for you: she is!"), female pride ("she holds her head up so high"), female identity ("I want to try on her clothes"), and female love ("I wanna be her best friend"). It's an intensely personal celebration of identity politics and cultural feminism, not a call to the barricades. There is revolution in it, but "the revolution is in her hips" — a clever pun and perhaps a reference to the alleged saying of some other early 20th-century feminist foremother: "If I can't dance, I don't want your revolution" (the quote has been wrongly ascribed to Emma Goldman). Bikini Kill liked their own song so much, they recorded and released it three times. It has been widely covered, including versions by Lutefisk and the Melvins with Teri Gender Bender. "Rebel Girl" became the most prominent anthem not just of Riot Grrrl but of third wave feminism. Thousands, if not millions, of girls and women took up its call for personal and cultural revolution, adopting the way that the song wrapped the common-sense ideas of feminism in a cloak of humor. And that chorus — the chorus that could be chanted, over and over.

Both Joe Hill's and Bikini Kill's songs capture key moments in the history of American resistance in the guise of odes to iconic muses. They both anchor their revolutionary moment in the body of a particular, strong woman. In "The Rebel Girl," Joe Hill was a man ahead of his time, pointing out the failure of inclusivity on the part of the IWW and the worker's rights movement. "Rebel Girl" takes feminism to the next stage of female empowerment: it is a song written mostly by women (the band shares writing credits), about women, for women. It's big, bold, explosive — one of the best punk rock songs ever. What really unites these Rebel Girls is the way both use inspirational figures to create inspirational songs. These rebel girls were not just imagined icons, they were lived experiences.

It's been 102 years since Hill's song, and 26 since Bikini Kill's. We live in a time when most of our top pop idols proudly declare themselves feminists. And yet the very alliance that Hill championed — between workers and women — helped cleave our country in 2016. Donald Trump defeated the first viable female presidential candidate in our country's 230-year history. Artists like Bruce Springsteen and Beyoncé publicly supported Hillary Clinton; Donald Trump couldn't get a single respected artist to perform at his inauguration. It's hard to believe in the possibility of meaningful protest music at this moment. But what choice do we have? A century ago, a few solid facts mixed with some humor and set to a memorable melody helped the workers of the world unite. Kathleen Hanna was just celebrating her friend Queen Juliana when she penned the anthem of an era. Sometimes change starts in the movement of a woman's hips. In 2017, Joe Hill was more right than ever: we must be sure to locate a few more Rebel Girls, because they are needed and needed badly.

WHAT EDUCATIONAL REVOLUTION LOOKS LIKE

JERVEY TERVALON

BACK IN THE LATE '70s, as a freshman at UC Santa Barbara, one of the guys on my dorm floor was surprised to hear that I had gone to Foshay Junior High in south Los Angeles. He said to me that his brother had taught there and had to learn to write on the chalkboard backward because he was afraid of turning his back to his students. He didn't have to finish his next sentence. I could fill in the gaps. His brother was worried about an eraser tossed at his head, or maybe being sucker-punched or even worse. Junior high is tough under the best of circumstances but in those years, for many of the kids Foshay was the worst of circumstances. Beatings and assaults, sexual and otherwise, took place with regularity between students, and sometimes violence was directed at the teachers. Guns were in lockers, and fear was thick on campus. What went on there was the leading edge of gang rules — "Crip here!" was heard in the halls and across the avenues.

In those years, I felt as though I had been committed to some kind of penal colony for unknown crimes. I read newspapers I picked up off lawns on my way to school or got lost in fat books — anything to escape the brutality of the situation. It didn't work. I was anxious about everything, even about the testing of the Klaxon sirens — maybe it wasn't the last Tuesday of the month, maybe we were going to be destroyed in a nuclear fireball. When I graduated from Foshay, I decided I would never return — I did my time and I was free to live out my days forgetting it.

That didn't work either. After I graduated from college, I returned home and decided to teach at Alain Leroy Locke High. Teachers and students at Locke faced many problems — the kids casualties of the blossoming cocaine epidemic and the steady state of gun violence to name a couple — but it all paled to what I had experienced at Foshay. Back then, it was like we were hermetically sealed into a mad world and no one outside could hear us crying and dying. I assumed that was because no one cared and the point was to get out or get dead. By the mid to late '80s, incremental steps to address school violence began to emerge. The schools still reflected the state of the communities — few jobs and many guns — but the situation had calmed ever so slightly. Locke felt like teaching in a state of low-grade anarchy with intermittent explosions of tragedy — as opposed to Foshay's live fire-zone feel — but I gave up on LAUSD and left for grad school to become a novelist and professor.

Now, decades later I'm on Foshay's campus again, or at the Saturday Academy at USC, bright and early in the morning at least once a week, working with black and Latino kids who are eager to read, to learn and be in an environment where personal safety isn't the overwhelming concern. I owe my lack of sleep to Kim Thomas-Barrios, the executive director of the USC-sponsored Neighborhood Academic Initiative, which she has lead since 2002. The NAI has me and many other black, white, Latinx, and Asian educators waking before dawn to teach at the Saturday Academy, which was started to provide more time on task in math, English, and SAT prep.

NAI is much more than just the impressive Saturday Academy. NAI directly addresses the economic and class isolation of communities of color. Just as I had done, those same African-American and Latino parents who made their way out of the working class and moved to more upscale neighborhoods exacerbated the hermetic isolation of working-class schools and communities. The success of NAI breaks down these class and race walls of isolation. Because the Saturday Academy is held at USC, these Latinx and African-American kids have the experience of studying on one of the most diverse campuses in the country. Kids will be kids, and some engage much more than others or in different ways. One of my 10th graders always wore a scowl, but she was the reader of the class — always with a new book and barely a spare word when I would ask her what she was reading. I was interrupting her flow … she needed to finish the test and get back to reading. I saw myself in her eyes, but she didn't have the fear I carried with me from those bad experiences so many decades ago because she was on the safe space of USC's campus. And even though Foshay's physical campus hasn't changed much in 40 years, it feels absolutely different: the teachers are as open and engaged as the students. Calculus graphs are posted outside of classrooms, and there is a feeling that the school is the center of the community. I've taught at almost all of the major universities in Los Angeles and I've had great students and not so great, but what really destroys the spirit of a teacher is the entitled student of means who believes they deserve a grade and refuse to engage or exert themselves. It is so refreshing to work with Foshay's students; the great majority show appreciation for the opportunities Foshay and NAI have provided them. Thomas Barrios has cultivated in these kids and their parents a culture of positive possibilities.

The success of Foshay is now entwined with the success of NAI, but it's important to recognize that the success of these programs is rooted in something more basic: the knowledge of how inner-city schools fail the students and community, as well as how inner-city schools are failed by systemic racism, mismanagement, and the lack of financial support. Maybe it's possible to recreate NAI's success, but you'd need to have a deep-pocketed, far-sighted institutional support such as USC's, and you'd need to find another Kim Thomas-Barrios: an inspiring, tireless leader from the community, who was born into a family that valued education more than anything else. Thomas-Barrios is a natural innovator who isn't in it for the money. She's here to show the world — with luck and relentless optimism — that you can help change for the better your block, your city, your world.

I'M THINKING ABOUT BUYING A GUN

DANEZ SMITH

my dreams are crowded with white
men's dreams, how empowered they feel
now that they can be racist in public again.
in my dreams all my blood & good as blood
are packed in my house, a new walled-in country.
children dance in the kitchen while we point guns
out the window until we grow magazines for thumbs
until we are the windows, sending lead prayers
into any "alt-right" out right nazi fuck who gets
too close with fire or laws. i don't want to
dream this but i have no say. don't want to
own a gun but if they come for my people
i'll be armed with more than pedagogy.
i don't have faith language will keep blood
in the body, mother in home, sister out of camp
my dreams, i tell you, they are metal warnings
loaded premonitions, nonsense that i can shot
holey until i see the truth in it. i pray i'm wrong
but i refuse to do all this blue weeping
when i should be learning to aim.
i practiced grief until i was its queen, so much
i reimagined the genre. i practiced grief
for too many moons, it's time to learn to shoot
to load a gun, to protect, to fight, to make a man

winged, to adorn him with silver in the lung.
these hands, they do work, but what's a hand to a trigger?
what peace is there for those called nigger?
called illegal? called sand nigger? called terrorist
by terrorist? i believe in nonviolence
but the people who hate me don't.
what good is a god your enemy won't bow to?
i. don't. want. to. own. a. gun. but. i. don't. want.
to. die. i chant peace peace peace peace peace
peace peace peace until i don't know
another word, until the word bleeds out.
i don't want to buy a gun.
i need to buy a gun.
i'd be dumb not to gun.
come, gun. come, metallic mercy.
come, my brand new man.
sweet nation of my blood.
i pledge to bang.

FREE SPEECH

DANEZ SMITH

a mouth a tongue a currency
a price a blood blot body like a word
a word a seed a dishonest fruit

a fruit of a mouth a fruit which explodes when it hits
a ground a ground scorched because
a man gave a word a word a rumor an order

a fire started with teeth a mouth
a rumor a lie a mob chasing
a boy a crime he didn't commit

a pattern a system a perpetual spell
a word a lie a gibberish curse an alternative fact
a revised light a lie alit

a censored prayer allah allah
a man says your body is no body
a man a lie a man says your god is not welcome

a lie a lie a war cry in the temple
a lie a burning fruit a snake's mouth a zombie dream
a word a directive agenda a king

a crown of red teeth a nazi a patriot
a racist a straight talker
a mask matching a face underneath

a mushroom cloud called a rose
a word a man a men amen when they mean
a me!me!me! a mess

a man saying you are a thing to weed
a garden of white chrysanthemum that hates
the dirt
a dirty word racism a word

a men don't want to be called
a word they are a word
are they waiting on a word? a signal?

how plainly stated can evil be?
make america great again
please, say exactly what you mean

say it with your whole mouth
your whole mouth a glove i dream
a dream of a room full of tongues

tongues are where god messed up
messed up if you think you slick
slick suit does not a good man make

man makes anything into a weapon
weapon has no synonym
i call you what you are

KENYATTA A.C HINKLE, *THE EVANESCED #130*, 2016, INDIA INK ON RECYCLED ACID FREE PAPER, 9 X 12 INCHES / COURTESY OF THE ARTIST

WAITING ON YOU TO DIE SO I CAN BE MYSELF

DANEZ SMITH

---

a thousand years of daughters then me
what else could i have learned to be?

girl after girl after giving herself to herself
one long ring shout name, monarchy of copper

& coal shoulders. the body too is a garment.
i learn this best from the snake angulating

out of her pork rind dress. i crawl out of myself
into myself, take refuge where i flee.

once, I snatched my heart out like a track
& found not a heart, but two girls forever

playing slide on a porch in my chest.
who knows how they keep count

they could be a single girl doubled
& joined at the hands. i'm stalling.

i want to say something without saying it
but there's no time. i'm waiting for a few folks

i love dearly to die so i can be myself.
please don't make me say who.

bitch, the garments i'd buy if my baby
wasn't alive. if they woke up at their wake

they might not recognize that woman
in the front making all that noise.

NO MORE COOKIES

REBECCA SCHIFF

This week Chelsea thinks she has colitis. Last week it was Lou Gehrig's disease. She's premed. She calls me every day from California to tell me her symptoms. She weeps about loose stools when her roommate is out of the room. Her roommate has a boyfriend, a bong, a Secret Service nickname. Nobody is kidnapping the roommate. Nobody is kidnapping Chelsea either, because she never leaves her room. Outside there are newspapers, cigar puns on the covers. Outside it's 72 degrees, and there's a World Bank protest at the campus center. There's her father's head sculpted in papier-mâché. Kids who will be lawyers in five years bang drums and kick a sack made of sand.

I pretend Huma is my daughter. If Huma had accompanied me to Africa last year, I wouldn't be up until three in the morning looking up dengue virus in the Physicians' Desk Reference. I wouldn't have to interrupt a noon meeting to remind Chelsea to go to lab. She cannot miss her labs, even if she's having diarrhea. There's got to be a bathroom in the science building, I tell her. She tells me that's not what the building is called. She hangs up on me, then calls me back a minute later to say she's sorry.

Huma doesn't use the bathroom. She comes to work fed, so I never see her snacking. The kitchen brings us snacks — clusters of grapes, low-cholesterol cheese on a round plate. Everything's round in this house, or oval. I bake cookies for my staff. It started as a joke, but Walter says I'm a natural. He says I can stay on as his pastry chef after Bill's term is over, which may be sooner than we think. I demur. I don't want to make tartufo for the Gores.

Between meetings, phone calls, negotiations, I bake. I bake lemon squares. I bake brownies. I overnight them to Chelsea so she has a reason to go to her postal box. Sometimes I enclose a folded article about how college depression can be beaten. Experts recommend exploring the surrounding area, taking day hikes. I wire her money for hiking boots.

"Dad and I will go with you the next time we come out there."

"The photographers will love that," she says. "First Family heals in sequoias.

Also, please stop sending baked goods. People with colitis shouldn't eat too much sugar."

"Give them to Megan," I say.

"What to Megan?"

"The biscotti I sent yesterday."

Chelsea starts crying.

"I think Megan gave us bed bugs. Her boyfriend has them."

"You wanted a roommate."

"I'm not good at making friends."

"You get that from me. Do the bites itch?"

I ask Huma to look up exterminators in Palo Alto. She comes back with a list of seven, ranked. We decide to quarantine Megan's boyfriend until the situation is resolved. I obtain his parents' address and Huma drafts a thank you note on East Wing stationery. We ask firmly that no one from the family speak to the press about the vermin. If Chelsea had her own boyfriend, we would ask the same.

The exterminator finds mouse droppings, but no bugs. Chelsea decides she has leptospirosis. She checks herself into the campus health center for 36 hours. She spends the entire time, as far as I can tell, watching *Buffy*. It's amazing anyone ever checks out.

Bill is keen to hike. He orders a book on Northern California's secret trails. He still thinks there's privacy on this earth for us, even now. He's having Teddy Roosevelt fantasies, roping off national parks in his mind. He wants it to be just the three of us, with helicopters overhead.

"She's a healthy young woman," he says. "She should be enjoying herself."

"Like other young women?"

"In her own way."

"Huma doesn't have fun," I say.

"Huma grew up in Saudi Arabia," he says. "She thinks leaving the house is fun."

"It wasn't like that for her. She went to British schools."

"Another group of people who really know how to have a good time."

Bill heads back into his wing, but he's still on all the TVs in mine.

What was it like for Huma? I ask her. Then I listen. I offer her blondies. She takes one to be polite, leaves most of it on her White House embossed napkin.

"Chelsea doesn't have the stomach for politics," I say, "so she's trying to be a doctor. But her stomach isn't letting her do that either. It's my fault."

"Her stomach is not your fault. I can mail her some breathing CDs."

"I don't know if I believe in breathing."

I believe in God. I believe in universal health care, in microcredit, in cunnilingus, and in dry cleaning. It doesn't matter what a first lady believes. I'll arrange a phone session for Chelsea with her father's pastor. I'll say she can talk to Huma. Huma lost her father and moved across the world. California isn't the Middle East. I've been to the Middle East. I've been to India and Bangladesh, Singapore, Rhodesia. Not anywhere, nowhere in the world, is a woman as free as Chelsea Clinton.

"It's Zimbabwe now, Mom," she says. "It hasn't been Rhodesia since 1980." She's taking a class on post-colonial history, another on post-feminist thought. All of her electives are posts. "But I like the idea of being free. I think I'm going to switch my major."

"To what?"

"Television Studies."

"You're going to major in television?"

"It's actually fascinating. Look what's happening to Dad."

I look up. There he is, a poof of white over a rosacea face, like a founding father who got a haircut. A second later, there's a passport photo of the girl with bangs, then the woman who snitched on her. I'm glad I have no friends. Post-feminism, there's less of a need.

"And the doctor at the health center said I should get tested for celiac disease. They have to do the tests off campus. Do I have insurance?"

"Everyone should have insurance in this country."

"Yes, agreed. But do I?"

"Of course you do. What is celiac disease?"

No more cookies, it turns out. No baklava when we're greeted in Greece. No cornbread at Thanksgiving, no stuffing. She can still eat the turkey, the one that didn't get pardoned. I've stopped watching the news. Walter is teaching me about rice flour, almond paste. We make many meringues now. I whip egg whites till they form soft peaks. Huma says they are delicious.

DANIELLE DEAN, *CON-TACT*, 2011, GRAPHITE ON PAPER, 17 X 13 3/4 INCHES / COURTESY THE ARTIST AND COMMONWEALTH AND COUNCIL, PHOTO: YONGHO KIM

COSMOPOLITAN PROJECTS: LONGISH POSTCARDS FROM A SHORT WEEK IN DETROIT

ANDREW DURBIN

September 2016

I.

They say many things about Detroit. Start with what this lanky kid says. He came bounding up to me at a bar close to the Wayne State campus, near where I was staying during a press trip organized by a privately funded cultural exchange program. He whispered: "Are you straight?" I said no. He said that was a shame because he's only into straight guys. His breath smelled sweetly of bourbon and Coca-Cola. He was so smashed he kept falling over himself as he rounded the pool table, trying to manage the cue without tripping over it, though twice it felled him. The straight guys laughed. A friend of his told me he's always like this. Like what? "Like he can hardly walk after midnight." It was sometime after one in the morning. Later he said, "Will you kiss me?" but I declined again, and instead we went across the street to an apartment complex with some other guy who was "definitely not voting for Clinton" because he was "sort of a Libertarian." I watched him and the kid smoke pot in a bathtub while college students played first-person shooter games in the darkened living room. Out of nowhere, the kid started to sob. He was lying on his back with his arms wrapped around his legs, as if he was trying to shrink himself down. When I asked what was wrong, he told me he couldn't afford to continue with his studies and had "no future." "That couldn't possibly be true," I assured him, that he had "no future." He held up his hand: "No, it is." His blue eyes were glassy and bloodshot from the booze and tears. I had no assurances to offer. I was just a visitor. Our host, who was doing just fine himself, understood. "It's true," he said, "it's hard to make it in Detroit."

This essay was originally commissioned for a publication that later rejected it because it criticizes one of its sponsors, the privately funded arts exchange that flew me out to Michigan for a week of openings, panel discussions, and guided tours. Its purpose, both then and now, is to make a brief observation of Detroit in September 2016. This was a peculiar time in the history of what was once among the largest cities in the United States. There was, for one, a distinct sense of relief in the air. For years, Detroit has been viewed as a something of a ghost town, the grand failure of American urbanism and industry, with a civic crisis occurring at an almost unbelievable scale and penetrating nearly every aspect of its citizens' lives. More recently, however, the city seems to have quietly slipped out of the news since it has been, tentatively speaking, undergoing a so-called renewal, or near renewal. Sometimes it's called a revitalization. Neither word seems quite right.

There also seemed, at least to my eye, to be fewer dire reports on the city's mismanagement and decline since the resignation of Kevyn Orr in 2014. Orr was appointed to the position of city manager by the governor after Mayor Kilpatrick was removed from office; his departure signaled a return to the democratic process. For a time, the people of Detroit had no say in their government. This wasn't the first time such a thing had happened (see the 1967 uprising, when the city underwent military occupation, now the subject of Kathryn Bigelow's *Detroit* [2017]) and probably won't be the last time. The governor declared the city's state of emergency over. The national focus was now on Flint, Michigan, where there was, and at the time of this writing still is, a water crisis.

By the time I got to Detroit in September 2016, we were careening toward the end of the presidential election in which Michigan ultimately played an unexpectedly decisive role in tipping the Electoral College in the Republican candidate's favor, ending for good the presidential ambitions of Hillary Clinton. Though I had never been to Michigan before and knew very little about the state, I was *certain* that Clinton would carry it and win the presidency — so much so that I frankly ignored the notes of indifference and hostility toward the Democrats that many Detroiters, both white and black, openly shared with me. Sure, Trump was awful but what about Clinton? What had she done for them? Most shrugged and said they were considering a third party vote for either Gary Johnson or Jill Stein, neither of whom seemed plausible to even the people who supported them. I often heard Detroiters ask what candidate would do for their city. I ignored what I heard about national politics. I did not believe that anecdotal evidence — my eye and my ear — was enough to signal that every Manhattan-based data journalist could be so wrong.

This essay consists mostly of anecdotes that do not attempt to make a larger argument about the situation on the ground in Detroit. It does not directly address the economic and political origins of decline or renewal, nor does it offer anything close to a complete portrait of the city. Instead, I've arranged a series of journal entries or longish postcards that follow the French writer and photographer Hervé Guibert's notion of "photographic writing," which he defined, in an appraisal of Goethe's late journals about his Italian travels, as a "staccato sketch" of a landscape with the "texture" of "photographic immediacy." This simpler and more direct writing, Guibert notes, differs from a normal fictional or even nonfictional account because it results from the brevity and transience of any observation made while traveling through a place that one will not stay at for long — and hardly knows. As such, it is a writing about impermanence and not-quite-knowing where one is.

In Detroit, I did not know where I was nor did I suspect that I would. I did not, after all, get into that bathtub.

II.

Detroit is the only city in the continental United States that's north of Canada. In this strange geographical confusion, there persists, at bottom, an existential awkwardness to this once-shining capital of American industry. A visitor is often set adrift in a locational ambiguity despite the help of our GPS-equipped phones, with little — building or landmark — serving to indicate where you are in the city at a given moment. By this I mean it's so large it's hard to fix your place in the sprawl. Usually, the tallest and best marker is the General Motors headquarters, with its lonely television eye atop its central tower, striking out against the vast Midwestern sky, but even this silvery complex sometimes disappears over the horizon. Beyond downtown, there's the storied run of fields and warehouses and a few still-standing neighborhoods in the blue mood of decline, some evidence of urban farming (though less than the internet would have you believe), and many large, unused buildings, like the city's gorgeous, defunct train station that was built by the same architects New York's Grand Central Station. Large segments of the city have crumbled, given way to ruin, or found themselves cordoned off, with neighborhoods islanded from one another through city-sanctioned demolition or insurance burnings. Since the collapse of the auto industry and subsequent bankruptcy led to the Detroit we know today, the city's economy is largely based on food manufacturing, some tech, higher education, small and intermittent business, the guy who owns Ohio-based Quicken Loans (and its real estate subsidiary, Black Rock), and casinos.

Connecting Detroit to Windsor, Canada, the Ambassador Bridge is the only privately owned bridge between the United States and its two neighbors. Built in 1927, it stretches 7,500 feet and is the busiest border crossing in North America, accounting for 60 to 70 percent of commercial truck traffic in the region. In 1979, a reclusive billionaire named Manuel Moroun purchased controlling shares of the bridge, and it has since been an important cudgel against Michigan in Maroun's disruptive real estate plans for the city. He has spent the last few decades buying up Detroit real estate for no reason, it seems, other than to stymie public projects. He owns the train station, but has no immediate plans for its use except to lease it out to film crews (talk of it becoming luxury apartments has ceased). He also purchased of the land along the river and, in the 2000s, even began to construct a second span of the Ambassador without notifying the Canadian government that he planned to expand his transit monopoly into their sovereign territory. Construction was halted when Canada got wind of the project, though I was told that the off-ramp still exists. The state would like to continue his project on its own terms, but Moroun refuses to sell his land to the city or state for those purposes. And so, traffic between the countries remains intractable.

I traveled to Detroit with a small group of artists, curators, and writers from several art and culture magazines, including *Cultured*, *ArtNET*, and *The Atlantic*. On the first day of our tour, which was conducted by a Detroit-based artist in a large rented van, we stopped at Michigan Central Station to admire its now-lost grandeur, as many locals encouraged us to do. At 18 stories, the station is the tallest building outside of downtown. It now stands in marked desolation on an empty parking lot colonized by weeds and surrounded by a tall barbed-wire fence equipped with security cameras, its classical facade vaguely redolent of Grand Central, with a set of four large doors set between a row of Corinthian columns. There is no way to visit the station's marble lobby, but recent ruin photography — a disagreeable genre for which Detroit is a favorite subject — reveals a grand stone concourse partially flooded and covered in huge swaths of graffiti, its windows shattered and walls largely gutted for salvageable material. Above the station's entrance, a rectangular office tower stands like the imposing wall of a fort, with its two towers linked by a span of windows, a doleful protectorate of broken train tracks.

In Detroit, the widespread sense of architectural and social loss is almost always accompanied by a sense of awe at what remains from those bygone days — and while some of the grand architectural evidence of that wealthier past, like the train station, has been spared demolition, much of it goes unused, with each site standing as a kind of large-scale memento mori for the city that was. Seen from almost anywhere downtown, the train station recalled, for me, the Acropolis in Athens: an ever visible monument to a lost era that remains totemic of the endurable spirit of the city. Outside the van, the air was tinged with an inexplicably boozy smell, as if a glass of Bourbon had been brought to my nose.

"Does it smell like whiskey?" *The Atlantic* writer asked. He threw his scarf around his neck as he said so, pulling out his small notepad in dramatic anticipation of the answer. "There's a distillery," our tour guide said, "just a mile or so away. The wind sometimes carries the smell."

We approached the security fence to get a better look at the station. Our guide told us he once broke in to take photographs (he is not a ruin photographer, he assured us; his artistic practice involves the documentation of inaccessible sculpture he places in forbidden or hard-to-reach sites such as the station), but since then Maroun has installed the fence and security cameras to keep out squatters, who are ubiquitous among the city's empty buildings and warehouses. He assured us that it is beautiful inside. Small knots of yellow flowers threaded through cracks in the pavement at our feet and in the few squares of grass in the parking lot, but otherwise the station is lifeless, a decrepit hunk of stone, concrete and marble.

There are many security fences in Detroit. Nearby, at the confluence of the Detroit and Rouge Rivers, a few miles from where the Ambassador Bridge extends to Canada, a former military base, Fort Wayne, sits behind one. The shuttered Fort was built, we were told, near once massive sand dunes that ran along the river, none of which are left. These dunes had been the thousand-year-old burial site of the native peoples of Detroit since before the French and American settlers arrived to claim the land for themselves (the precise tribe responsible for these burial sites is unknown, though the land was later claimed by the Potawatomi). By the 1950s, the auto industry had harvested most of the sand for windshields, leaving one rather small mound behind, surrounded by barbed-wire fence, as an unmarked memorial to the dead who were turned into glass for the midcentury commuter.

III.

We shuttled between panels, museums, galleries, cultural initiatives, talks, dinners, a few lunches, hotels, trendy cafes, a mural project that paired kids with their elderly neighbors, DIY art projects and installations, with detours to many of Detroit's emptier neighborhoods to visit with activists who were working to improve daily life in the city. I struggled to find the words to describe these places. Each was imbued with a particular kind of energy. At some point, someone from out of town said, "There's a lot of potential here." In fact, there were people there, people who had been there for quite some time and who were, through a variety of community-based strategies, attempting to do something good for their knackered city. "Potential" had nothing to do with it. The word irked me.

At one panel — a discussion on art and progress — in a warehouse-turned-artist-studios one evening, a black woman interrupted a speaker after he used the word "abandoned" to describe some part of the city. She stood up and seized a microphone to voice her opposition to that word — "abandoned" — which, she argued, is intrinsically connected to whiteness in its assumption that the absence of white bodies and white history suggests that the people who occupy those places, whether they live there now or not, were not, are not, and never will be "there." The panelists, who nodded in agreement, were silent as she spoke. She said she had lived in the city her whole life and the influx of people who didn't actually know the city bothered her. The audience clapped. There-ness, she suggested, is itself a white construct in the white-centered imaginary of Detroit, because who gets to say who's there, except white people. "Nowhere in Detroit is abandoned," she said.

ELANA MANN, *THE ASSONANT ARMORY* (INSTALLATION VIEW), 2016, DETAIL OF THE EAR PEDESTAL AND THE HANDS-UP-DON'T-SHOOT-HORN / COURTESY THE ARTIST AND COMMONWEALTH AND COUNCIL, PHOTO: JEAN-PAUL LEONARD

I opened my notebook as the panel resumed, reviewed some of the observations I had made about Detroit, and cringed at own thoughtless vocabulary for post-industrial cities and the American Midwest, a vocabulary I had inherited from the touristic disaster journalism of the last decade or so. "Abandoned," "apocalyptic," "destroyed," "bombed out" were deployed by visitors on my tour to describe places we had never been to before and, in many cases, didn't even get out of the car to observe closely for ourselves. I had copied down those words too, adding "ruined," "voided," and "wiped out." I struck each from the pages of my small black notebook, stopping at "desolate," which means, in the original Latin, "thoroughly alone." That word suited much of the city and its sprawl of parking lots, neighborhoods, and former centers of town (Detroit, like Los Angeles, is dispersed across a network of communal nodes, townships-of-a-sort folded into a larger, quasi-cohesive urbanity). Much of Detroit is thoroughly alone, cut off from itself and from the aid of the country it helped to produce.

In some instances, these desolate areas are so isolated that they appear sealed off, enclosed in a translucent bubble that seemingly divides them from the rest of the city. Boynton, for example, is a mostly demolished neighborhood near the Marathon Petroleum Refinery. The Refinery — a wide, hulking colossus of tubes and spires spewing white smoke into the air — now works with highly toxic tar sands rather than conventional oil. Several years ago, Marathon bought out and bulldozed many of the nearby houses, though some still stand in threadbare lots separated far apart from one another. These last holdouts are now unsellable since many have been valued, as of 2014, at less than $16,000 per home. Known as Detroit's "dirtiest zip code," Boynton also has the highest cancer rate in Michigan. The foul air around the neighborhood reeks of a nauseating chemical smell that bears no resemblance to anything I had ever encountered before. It was the acrid, indescribable smell of cancer — and of failure. Tar sands, and the chemicals used to dilute the fuel so it can move through pipelines, like benzene, are highly carcinogenic, and the industry is mostly unregulated in the United States and Canada, where the sands are harvested at enormous ecological cost.

IV.

After the panel discussion on art and progress, some of us — the panelists, a few local gallerists, curators, and writers — were conveyed across the city to Wasserman Projects, a 9,000-square foot art gallery housed in an old fire station in the Eastern Market neighborhood. In the dark, it was difficult to tell where we stood in relation to the rest of the city; someone smoking outside said we weren't far from downtown, though it seemed as if we had been dumped in a field in the middle of the state. Across the street, white trucks lined the rear of a depot for Roscoe & Horkey Farms. Despite our extensive cultural tour, which included the Museum of Contemporary Art and the Detroit Institute of the Arts, I was still unsure of what the city's art scene was like, and I hoped Wasserman Projects would provide some idea of its shape.

The Projects is massive. I tried to take a picture with my phone, but my camera couldn't capture its shadowy vastness as it extended into a dark, grassy field. We could have been standing in the middle of nowhere but we were somewhere, under a moonless night sky splashed with thousands of stars. The city's light pollution wasn't so bad, much better than in New York, and I could make out the slight shapes of a few constellations: Cygnus, the swan; the little and the large bears; Lyra, the harp. I wondered about the kid in the bathtub and where he might be, whether he was back at the bar near Wayne State, begging strangers to kiss him as he orbited the porch under this same sky. No one is abandoned in Detroit.

Inside the gallery, three wire cages loomed in the large main space, surrounded by an improbable array of chicken-themed art and a few makeshifts bars and tables, all hazily lit by soft overhead light. Two of the coops were filled with adult chickens clucking on a bed of sawdust, while the other held several hundred eggs. In an adjacent room, hundreds of chicks clustered under heat lamps. Waiters scurried around with drinks and hors d'oeuvres. One stopped in front me and said, "Welcome to Koen Vanmechelen's cosmopolitan chicken project," meaning the show, which was technically called *Energy/Mass*.

"Excuse me?"

He handed me a pink gin cocktail that had been thickened with egg whites. He noted this in case I was vegan. I am not. "Good," he said. "Because dinner is chicken." The artist Adam Pendleton, who had spoken on that evening's panel, looked stunned when he considered the room before us. Then he broke into laughter: "Chickens?"

A cryptic press release explained that the exhibition was "the newest phase of Vanmechelen's ongoing, 20-year-long Cosmopolitan Chicken Project (CCP), which cross-breeds chickens from around the world as a means of exploring cultural, biological, and aesthetic diversity." The chickens, seen in cages around the gallery, were the result of this "cosmopolitan project" and were to be given to the city's farmers. *Energy/Mass* included several bizarre sculptures and photographs, including a metal sword with a black chicken posed on top; a few votive arrangements of stuffed chickens placed alongside portraits of chickens; some large photographs of chickens as well as one of the artist blowing smoke in the shape of a chicken's egg; two light-box sculptures of the words "energy" and "mass"; and several books containing his breed's genetic code.

In the main room, the gallery had arranged long, narrow white tables in an L-shape around the three coops. Cartons of eggs were stacked in the tables' centers, with a single egg placed before each setting with a guest's name written on it. I found my name near Adam Pendleton and the artist Trevor Paglen.

"I think we're going to eat the chickens," Adam said.

"While looking at them?" I asked.

While we were looking at them.

We took our seats. Before dinner, Vanmechelen, a middle-aged Belgian man with a Flemish accent and a thick mustache and tousled hair, stood up and thanked us for coming to his show and described, in brief, how much these chickens meant to him, how he had been breeding them for decades as a gift to the city that he called home. I was seated beside a woman who worked for the municipal department responsible for liaisoning with the city's urban farmers. As the artist spoke at length about his chickens, she told me that, while there were many urban farmers in the city, few were approved by the city (her department was simply too small to regulate livestock) and none had yet been allowed to raise any animals, though many did

— illegally. The cosmopolitan chicken would be the city's official chicken and she was already working with some farmers, including an older man who sat opposite us, to introduce the bird to the city.

The farmer said hello, but little else. "He's modest about his work," the city worker told me, beaming at her friend, who was hunched over a plate of food. While we talked about urban farming, the gallery served us mustard greens from his farm. The city worker had known the urban farmer for many years, and she said he was both a good friend and an integral part of her community. He often provided food for large picnics that she attended with her husband, who sat beside her and who nodded at me when I introduced myself. (The men's silence was cordial and seemed to belong to the manners of a more introspective age.) She showed me photos on her phone: in one, a group of about 12 men, women, and children stood before a long table covered with salads, meats, and other dishes. This work made the woman sincerely happy, she beamed as she flicked through the images on her photos app, though she told me she was also thinking of retiring soon and moving south (where I am from). She was concerned however about racism and the intransigent anti-blackness of the Southern states' governments. The South — South Carolina and Georgia, specifically — worried her. She doubted she would leave. Her children still lived in Detroit.

The urban farmer ate quietly while we spoke. Later, our tour guide joined us for dessert and we continued to discuss city planning, urban farming, and the famous investor in Detroit's future, Dan Gilbert of Quicken Loans. Gilbert's real estate subsidiary Bedrock had partially funded — it funds almost everything now — my trip to Detroit. Through his two companies, Gilbert has poured massive amounts of cash into the city, both in real estate holdings and in cultural initiatives, making him *the* dominant force in city life since the 2008 crash and 2013 city bankruptcy.

Sensing that I distrusted Gilbert's philanthropy, our tour guide told us he didn't care where, or how, the money got to Detroit, as long as it got there. I wondered aloud if the reliance on predatory capitalism to fund the city's revitalization, if that's the word, might not restage the exact problems that have plagued Detroit for a century.

His face was blank. Yes, and no, he conceded.

Quicken Loans, according to *The New York Times,* is the second largest mortgage lender in the United States. Its business is "the selling of the American Dream" to the American people, whatever that means, and this business once attracted the attention of the Obama-era Justice Department, which accused the company of misrepresenting "borrowers' income or credit scores, or inflated appraisals, in order to qualify for Federal Housing Administration insurance. As a result, when those loans soured, the government says that taxpayers — not Quicken loans — suffered millions of dollars in losses."

I argued that Gilbert was a false prophet of Detroit's future: hurting the poor and underserved to enrich the wealthy while appealing to a disintegrating middle class through art. While he was responsible for the comeback of downtown (mostly through swanky and largely unaffordable restaurants), outside of the gentrified sectors, people were in need of food and basic services. At a Bedrock-funded opening for an exhibition by the artist Gary Simmons, several apparently homeless people gathered near the door to ask for money and food. Their presence and number cast the event in stark terms, rendering the economic privileges afforded by the mostly white crowd and the out-of-towners that much more visible. The dynamic between the crowd inside and the crowd outside highlighted the drastic inequality that shaped the city — and that Gilbert not only helped produce, but actively exploited for personal gain. We were drinking champagne in plastic flutes while the people standing outside were struggling to afford a meal.

Our tour guide remained unconvinced and, in any case, dessert was served. The city worker had no comment and the urban farmer wasn't listening.

V.

In the last few years, the question of the American Dream has become a leading theme in the Midwest: is there such a thing anymore?

For the sake of argument, I won't consider here its dependency on a white imaginary of ownership, space, and ambition and whether it ever existed at all. Let's accept the essential assumption that it did or does, if only as a postwar rhetorical strategy for expansionist economic policy. Let's say the fiction matters, and that it matters particularly in a place like Detroit. In the openly racist, anti-Semitic, conspiratorial Republican talking points of the past year or so, Barack Obama had either sold the public out and personally destroyed the Dream in retaliation against past American imperialism or was in cahoots with an international Jewish banking conspiracy to ensure that Dream was priced out of the hardscrabble everyman's imaginative budget. George Soros, and the Witch of Chappaqua (who is a gentile and a Methodist) were all leading culprits in this crooked scheme, of course (see President Trump's final "Argument for America" ad). Indeed, Detroit — and many of America's inner cities, which the Republican candidate frequently and erroneously described as "war zones" — became, once again, ground zero for those failures. (Trump took up this theme once more in his feeble Inaugural speech, again citing Detroit.)

The brain surgeon Ben Carson, a Detroit native, led Donald Trump on a five-minute (yes, really) tour of the city's southwest, to show the nominee what, and where, things had gone wrong. In their eyes, free trade, regulation, "P.C. values," cheap heroin and other drugs ferried across our unprotected border with Mexico, as well as Democratic electoral dominance were, of course, the inevitable culprits in the demise of the Rust Belt. The impoverished belt itself had expanded well beyond its original borders, stretching across most of the middle of the country, from the tip of the Great Lakes, down along the Mississippi and into the post-industrial Deep South, all of which would become the rotund electoral bloc that would ensure Trump's November win. The decline of federal aid and subsidies, corporate tax loopholes, and the rapid growth of the one-percent class at the expense of everyone else, were not included on Dr. Carson and Mr. Trump's menu of possible causes for what they themselves conceded was the nightmare their constituents were living.

After his Carson-led dalliance through the "war zone," Trump gave a maudlin speech "from the heart" at the Great Faith Ministries, a historic black church in Detroit. He promised that if he were to become president, "tomorrow will be better." He also reminded his suspicious audience that Abraham Lincoln was a Republican, apparently in an attempt to link himself to the centuries-long struggle for emancipation and equal rights. Or something. Trump himself seemed unsure about why he brought up Lincoln. Who, in any case, had forgotten? But, more to the point, whose tomorrow?

Today's Republicans, and some of today's liberals were right to pose their question in Detroit, the patient zero of the Great American Slowdown. Like the question itself, the Detroit to which this question is posed is itself a fiction, a flickering and impermanent image on the nationalist screen, resulting not from fact but, rather, from a set of erroneous assumptions. There is, after all, no war zone, no matter what Trump imagines. There is, however, a city built of — and for — impermanent and highly destructive industries. There is a city torn apart by the misuse of public funds, the electioneering of the far right, the privatization-pushes of local and state governments in Michigan and across the United States. There is a city beholden to the wonky generosity of billionaires who have, generally, used their substantial income to subvert any effort to actually remedy Detroit's problems, like supporting a meaningful reform of the tax system, which might strengthen and expand the safety net or increase funding for public schools and not voucher programs. (The president's school-choice-focused Education Secretary, Betsy DeVos, is from Michigan.) The city's difficulties are not so much rooted in a lack of jobs as in a failure of the neoliberal order that produced both the city *and* Donald J. Trump.

What is the American Dream if clean water is hard to come by, as it is in Flint? What is the Dream if one lives under the poison cloud of tar sands plant? *These* are the problems of the Midwest, *these* are the problems of the American Dream, and yet those who keep pushing us to "make it great again," who tweet the imbecilic promise of some new and soon-to-arrive Dream, are the very same people who stand to gain the most from maintaining or even heightening the crisis of its grim reality. Their question — whatever happened to the American Dream? — is as perverse as the president who poses it, and it is in recognition of this perversity that we might learn to distrust both equally.

Detroit is the best representative of the state of that Dream today, absent still from the heads of workers and ex-union members, the under- or not employed, those used and forgotten by the industries that created and destroyed the city. In Detroit, it is not so much that the Dream has died as it has been reduced to its rawest form, limited in its imaginative scope to the teapot tycoons who run the show now: loan sharks, casino magnates, the owner of a bridge to nowhere. These are our so-called Dreamers, who dream of possession and subjugation, of voter suppression and natural gas; it is the Dream that the lot of available stuff, cash and goods, properties and cities, belong to a mere few, a few whose anemic hope is the hope of protection from those forces that would seek to *redistribute*, to *take back*, to *take away*, to *share*, and to *overthrow*. The American Dream is, in the end, no dream at all but instead a flimsy, unconvincing fiction. So be it.

If Detroit offers us any true dream, one that we might strive to bring into reality, it might be the dream of an abnegated America in which we might someday find a usable future rather than the fantasy of a past.

VI.

In the bowels of the Detroit Institute of the Arts lies one of the world's great conservation departments. The conservators are employed by the museum and by private collectors as well as other institutions, so our tour was asked not to write about or photograph any of the works we saw. This rule applied to contemporary art and works dating back to the early Middle Ages alike — the danger was that they might not belong to the DIA. There were several astonishing pieces in the department, including a work by a contemporary artist who was, in light of a recent solo retrospective at a gallery on Manhattan's Upper East Side, a name everyone was discussing at the time. Even the *Atlantic* writer, who seemed indifferent to art of any kind, recognized this artist's work and admitted, or at least feigned, awe at the presence of a rare, previously unknown sculpture. In any case, we saw many things: tattered, aged, newly cleaned-up objects; objects in storage, objects in photographs, objects wrapped in plastic, objects I can't name here but recognized as objects made by famous object-makers.

In a forensic room, where pieces were photographed using scientific cameras, we were invited to see X-rays of a medieval wooden statue of a Virgin and Child. The sculpture was from Galicia, I think, or at least somewhere in Spain, and had been in the possession of a small village until it ended up with some unknown person or institution or the DIA itself — the conservator would not or could not divulge its provenance. It was visible to the tour only as a luminous negative, printed in a loose grid of smaller X-rays that had been arranged into a scaled image of the sculpture. Before us, the Virgin took her shape on a light-box installed on the wall opposite the X-ray camera, a clumsily hung image of the real thing, which was at an off-site storage facility. Outlined in stark white, her innards were largely dark — hollow — except for a few bright streaks at the lines that defined the Child, her dress, her features, her arms. She stood less like a Christian figure than a kind of map, its white lines representing a patchwork of crisscrossing roads.

"What do you notice about this?" the conservator asked us.

The eyes were different, perfectly circular, as if they had been carved separately and were inserted (that was the case: they were glass). Otherwise, the sculpture had been penetrated throughout by small, white pricks about the length of the pinky finger.

"The nails?" someone asked.

"The nails, yes," the conservator replied. "But what about them?"

None of us knew what to say, so he explained that the straighter nails were modern — and had been manufactured by machine — while the crooked, irregular nails were much older since they had been made by hand. He said that we could tell a lot about a sculpture's origins based on details such as these nails. We can tell what might have needed repair, and when those repairs were made. We can even tell what might have caused the damage. We can tell if something was dropped, burned, or if parts were replaced — however seamless the replacement appears on the surface. Such small things, he explained, contain the history of an object and, in turn, contain the history of the place that made the object. These histories overlap and revise one another, leaving us with this: the sculpture.

"Where will it go after it's been repaired?"

"Somewhere else. In the meantime, you can see it here." What was there was a negative, an

X-ray, light in a dark room.

I asked him what these nails told him about the sculpture and its village. He said he did not yet know.

VII.

On my final night in the city, I returned to the bar near the Wayne State Campus in search of the lanky kid. The other writers were still at a dinner for an artist at a newish downtown restaurant. I left early after I found myself seated next to three Republican donors to the cultural exchange program, who were telling me about the sad state of public education and why they supported "school choice." I excused myself to go to the restroom and instead exited the restaurant, into a breezy evening. My cab took me uptown, through the lonely expanse of interstate roads, back to the university, and circled awhile as I tried to remember where the bar was. It had been somewhat close to the Institute of the Arts, but this wasn't much help to the driver. "We can do this all night," the driver said, "or you can just Google it."

I Googled it. "Just let me out here," I said when we arrived near a recognizable administration building. I walked a bit, looked for the bar, found none, debated returning to my hotel, turned a corner, and there it was, the bar where I had been told nobody was going to vote for Hillary Clinton or Donald Trump. It was midnight, a few college students lounged on its wraparound porch smoking and drinking beer, whispering to one another. The bar vibrated with pop music while outside the city was becalmed by a strange silence, as if we had been placed under a glass dome. I hadn't wanted to feel so apart but I was, more so than I had ever felt in any other American city, and I couldn't explain it to myself, why I could not penetrate Detroit — or ever feel like I had landed. Rather, I remained aloft, despite every effort I made to drop down to earth. Even here, where I had come closest to the city, I felt as if I still hovered slightly off the ground.

Detroit has accrued such myth, of both its success and its failure, and it seemed buried alive in expectation — though of what I didn't even know. War zones and squats, hip cafes and urban farms. There was a flat Midwestern melancholy to everything, but was that simply the eerie start of fall, with its brisk nights and starry skies? Had I invented the mood for it? Was it mine? Or was it simply the city's reality, reality as a postscript to the American century it had singularly helped to ensure.

The bartender served me a vodka on ice. The cubes cracked as the liquid settled into the glass. No one was at the pool table and everyone was outside. I wasn't sure if I had actually come to see the kid again or not, what I had to say or what I wanted to ask, but regardless he was not there and would not come. It was near closing time. The bar would soon empty out and the implacable night would eventually become day. The bar would soon empty out and the implacable night would eventually become day and a small plane would take me into its belly and fly me back to New York.

EXTRAORDINARY AND PLENIPOTENTIARY

HOOMAN MAJD

THE AMBASSADOR ARRIVED at the Chancery at exactly nine in the morning, as was his custom. He walked past the receptionist, tilting his head in a way that left the gesture open to interpretation. It could have been a greeting or a nervous tick. The ambassador, in his mid-50s, balding and slightly overweight, walked with a confidence that bordered on arrogance, heading for his office, which was situated at the end of a long hallway. He muttered an inaudible greeting to his secretary who was seated at a small desk outside his door, and quickly stepped into his private suite. The secretary stood up, straightened her skirt, adjusted her top and followed him inside.

"Sir?" Nervously, she watched his movements.

"Yes?" He pulled out a large leather wing chair and sat down behind his desk. He opened the lowest drawer and picked up a half-empty bottle of scotch.

"Sir, a telex came in last night."

"Read it to me." The ambassador unscrewed the bottle cap and leaned across his desk for a glass.

"It's coded, sir. '*Top Secret.*'"

"Well, get Salehi to decode it." The ambassador poured himself a generous shot of whiskey.

"He's not in yet, sir, but if you give me the keys I'll fetch the code book for you."

"It's not necessary," said the ambassador, taking a sip. He grimaced slightly. "The revolution can wait for Salehi." He put his glass down. "Anything else *azizam*?"

"Yes, sir. The Foreign Ministry has called twice but they wouldn't tell me what it's about."

"Which Foreign Ministry? Theirs or ours?" The ambassador took another sip of whiskey.

"Theirs. Shall I call them back?"

"No, let them wait." The ambassador drained his glass and reached across the desk and lifted the lid of an intricately engraved silver cigarette box.

"Close the door behind you."

Leaning back in his chair, he lit a Winston and stared at the large framed photograph of the Shah hanging on the opposite wall. He hadn't bothered to take it down yet. The Shah, wearing a resplendent uniform with a myriad of medals pinned to his chest, stared back more glumly than usual. The ambassador sat motionless for a few moments and then poured himself another shot. He lifted the glass and turned it with his fingers until the Imperial Seal faced him. He examined the seal, and then looked at the Shah again.

"*Be-salaamati*," he said bitterly, *to your health*. "A lot of good those medals did you. And thanks for leaving your friends behind to rot." He took a sip and crushed his cigarette out on the raised seal of the ashtray in front of him. "You son-of-a-bitch." He then picked up a newspaper from two days ago, airmailed from Miami. Iran was once again on the front page. A knock at the door interrupted him. Mr. Salehi, Deputy Chief of Mission and the only other diplomat assigned and accredited to this tiny embassy — a distant outpost in a Latin American country hardly any Iranian knew existed — poked his head in.

"M-may I c-come in sir?"

"Come in Salehi," said the ambassador, looking up from his paper. "And stop that stammering, for God's sake. This new government will crucify you if they hear you speak!"

"I c-can't help it, sir," said Salehi. "It's g-gotten worse s-since the troubles."

"Troubles? Is that what you call this 'glorious' revolution? I wouldn't repeat that around Tehran ears, if I were you. Do you want a drink?"

"N-no, thank you sir. I have the t-telex de-de-c-c-coded, sir."

"What does our illustrious new government have to say this fine morning?"

"*Chashm, ghorboun*." Salehi cleared his throat. "*Be' arze' agha-ye...*"

"Yes, yes, yes," said the ambassador. "Just read the important parts."

Salehi cleared his throat again. "THE FOREIGN MINISTER OF THE PROVISIONAL REVOLUTIONARY GOVERNMENT REQUESTS YOUR PRESENCE IN TEHRAN AT THE FOREIGN MINISTRY NO LATER THAN THE THIRTIETH OF ESFAND STOP INFORM HOST MINISTER OF INTENTION TO WITHDRAW YOUR CREDENTIALS STOP M SALEHI TO ACT AS INTERIM CHARGE DAFFAIRS STOP REQUEST YOU ADMIT LOCAL IRANIAN RESIDENTS TO PROTECT REVOLUTIONARY GOVERNMENT INTERESTS STOP REQUEST IMMEDIATE REPLY STOP. It's s-signed off by the new m-minister, s-sir."

The ambassador poured himself another large drink. "We knew it was coming, didn't we?" He gestured for Salehi to sit down and took a gulp from his glass. "Do you want a drink?"

"*N-na merci*, sir." Salehi seemed to just drop into one of the overstuffed armchairs in front of the ambassador's desk. "S-sir, what are you going to do n-now?"

The ambassador's phone rang.

"*Baleh*?"

"Sir, it's the Foreign Ministry again," his secretary's voice came from the receiver. "The Acting Deputy Foreign Minister for the Middle East: shall I put him through?"

"No, no. Salehi will call him back. No more calls!" He hung up and turned to Salehi. "Well," he said, "looks like we'll have to find ourselves an Iranian who wants this damn embassy. In the meantime, make me up a new civilian passport and send it over to the American Embassy for a visa. I think I'll go to Washington. The Americans fucking owe us — the Brits more, but London is full of fucking Arabs."

"Yes, s-sir. But who should I call? I m-mean, to admit to the embassy."

"How should I know! You know all the Iranians here; you decide. You're in charge now, Salehi."

"Well, s-sir, there are only three Iranians here, and two are Baha'is. I shouldn't think they'd want to get involved, would they?"

"Don't be ridiculous." The ambassador gave him a dirty look. "Who's the third?"

"M-Mohammad Ali Shirazi, s-sir. He's been here a couple of t-times, to the p-parties. B-but I'm not sure what he d-does, sir."

"He'll be fine with a name like that. Call him and get him over here. And get me my American visa." The ambassador stood up. "Come on Salehi, get to work. My passport photos are in the desk outside, and now I'm going back to the Residence."

Salehi stood up and followed the ambassador out the door and down the hall to his own office, the only other office in the embassy. Suddenly the ambassador stopped, turned, and put his hand on Salehi's shoulder. "Reply to the telex, will you?" he said. "Say whatever you want." He paused for a moment, looking into Salehi's eyes for the first time in the many years they had worked together. "Salehi, either I'll — maybe we — have two or three or six months to ponder country, faith, honor — what we did, what our sins were. Who knows how long these clowns can actually stay in control. Or, as I suspect is possible, given how wily an ayatollah can be, I'll have the rest of my life to do just that. Like the Russians in Paris 60 years ago." He turned again. "Oh, and just call the fucking Deputy Minister here in this godforsaken place they call a country, whatever his fucking name is, would you?"

The ambassador then nodded his head at the receptionist, and walked out the door of the Chancery building.

Salehi sat down at his desk and held his head in his hands. He sat like that for a few minutes and then slowly lifted his head, hands still on his cheeks. He stared at the blank white space on the wall where the Shah's photograph had been until a few days ago. Chargé D'affaires *indeed*, he thought. He pulled open a drawer and thumbed through some thin files, selected one, and opened it. He picked up the phone and dialed a number. A sleepy female voice answered. "Señor Shirazi, *por favor*," he said.

"*Perdón*?"

"M-Mohammad Ali Shirazi, *p-por f-favor*." There was a brief silence.

"Sí," a man's voice boomed into the receiver.

"*Agha-ye* Sh-Shirazi?" asked Salehi.

"*Baleh*?"

"*S-Salaam*; it's Salehi, f-from the embassy. Did I wake you up?"

"No, no; it's okay. Anything wrong? News from Tehran?"

"I was w-wondering if you could c-come b-by the embassy t-t-today. I have s-something t-to discuss with you."

"Why?" said Shirazi.

"It's this re-revolution, you know. I have t-to talk with you."

"Okay..." Shirazi hesitated. "What time?"

"Well, as s-soon as p-possible."

"I'll come by in a couple of hours."

"*M-Merci*, Agha-ye Shirazi."

Salehi hung up and then quickly dialed the secretary. "C-could you get me the Deputy M-Minister, please?" he asked. "And then p-please c-come into my office?"

He replaced the receiver and turned in his swivel chair to face the safe on the floor behind him. He opened it and took out the ambassador's diplomatic passport and a stack of blank civilian passports. He turned back to his desk, and carefully copied the ambassador's details into a blank passport by hand. When finished, he took a rubber stamp from his drawer, inked it, and pressed it on the top of the front page, over the words "Imperial Government of Iran" and the lion-and-sword government seal. He stared at the crude red letters for a moment, "Provisional Revolutionary Government of Iran," and then turned back to the safe and retrieved his own diplomatic passport. He started to make a passport for himself when the phone rang. "*Baleh*?" he said.

"I have the Deputy Minister on the line, Mr. Salehi," said the secretary.

"*M-Merci, khanoom*," said Salehi. He held the receiver tightly in his hand. "Your

Excellency, it's F-First S-Secretary Salehi."

"Good morning, Mr. Salehi. We've been trying to reach His Excellency the ambassador all morning. We've had indications from a friend in Tehran that he has been recalled. Of course, we haven't had official notice yet."

"N-No, Your Excellency, t-that will b-be c-communicated shortly, I'm sure. I'll be acting as Chargé until a new ambassador is ap-appointed."

"When will the ambassador be leaving us?" asked the Deputy Minister.

"I'll inform you p-personally as s-soon as His Excellency's p-plans are f-finalized."

"Thank you, Mr. Salehi. I'd like to see you at your convenience, after the ambassador departs, of course."

"I'll be sure and m-make an ap-appointment, sir. G-Goodbye, Your Excellency."

Salehi hung up the phone, wiped his sweaty palms on his handkerchief, and resumed working on his passport. The knock on the door startled him. He stuffed his handkerchief back in his breast pocket and sat up straight in his chair. "Come in, p-please," he said loudly. The door opened and the secretary walked in.

"You wanted to see me?" she asked, smoothing her skirt again with a sharp brush of her hand.

"Yes, yes," said Salehi standing up. "P-please; sit down."

"Is anything wrong?" asked the secretary, slowly lowering herself into the metal chair. Salehi stood behind his desk for a while, his hands in his pockets.

"N-No," he said, as he sat down. "Actually, y-yes. There is s-something wrong. The ambassador's been recalled." The secretary stared at him. "And I'm the Ch-Chargé until a n-new ambassador is assigned." He looked at the passports on his desk. "C-Can you b-bring me the ambassador's p-passport photos?"

"Yes, sir," said the secretary, slowly getting up. She walked to the door, stopped, and turned. "What's going to happen to us, sir?" she asked, turning again. She walked out of the office without waiting for the answer. Salehi went back to his passport, finishing with the rubber stamp on the front page, and then he carefully glued a black-and-white photo of himself on the third page. He embossed the photo with a heavy seal, examining his handiwork with some pleasure. A knock startled him again, and the secretary walked in. "Here's the ambassador's photo," she said, holding out a small glassine envelope. Her eyes were wet.

"Thank you," said Salehi. "P-please; have a seat. This won't t-take a m-minute." Salehi glued and sealed the ambassador's photo onto his new passport, put it and his own passport in a manila envelope, and turned to the secretary. "C-Could you s-send these over to the American Embassy? For v visas? Ask for extended multiple-entry ones, please."

"Yes, sir." She stared at Salehi as she took the envelope from his hand.

"Oh," said Salehi, "and a Mr. Sh-Shirazi will be coming to s-see m-me this m-morning. I think you've m-met him. He'll be working at the embassy for a while, in an unofficial ca-capacity." Salehi rubbed his hands on his trousers.

"Will that be all, sir?"

"*Baleh, khanoom*," replied Salehi. "*M-Merci.*" The secretary walked out of the office and hurried to her desk. She picked up the phone and rang the embassy chauffeur, thumbing through the two new passports in her hands.

"Come to the ambassador's office," she said when the chauffeur finally answered. "You need to go to the American Embassy — the Consular section." She hung up and lit a Vantage cigarette; rumor in Tehran was that this was what the Empress smoked, airlifted from the embassy in Washington to *Niavaran* palace by the crate every month. She put the passports back in the manila envelope and then opened her desk drawer and took out her own, a civilian one with a little over a year's validity left. She thumbed through it before putting it in the envelope with the other two, and then picked up the phone and dialed the US Embassy.

"Consular Section," a voice said after a few rings.

"Good morning," said the secretary, in as sweet a voice as she could manage. "I'm calling from the Iranian ambassador's office. We'll be sending over three passports for visas — just tourist or visitor visas — directly to the Consul's attention. Could you please let him know?"

"The Consul's not available now, ma'am, but I'll let him know as soon as he's back in his office. The *Iranian* ambassador, you said?"

"Yes," said the secretary. "That's correct."

"And when does he need a visa?"

"*We* need the visas as soon as possible, please," said the secretary.

"I'll let the Consul know, ma'am. He'll call you if there are any questions or issues. He may want to speak with the ambassador."

"Thank you." The secretary hung up the phone and put out her cigarette. She quickly typed a letter on official stationary, still with the imperial lion-and-sword seal, and signed the ambassador's name. She put it in the envelope with the passports, picked up the phone and dialed the Residence. "Is the ambassador there, Maria?" she asked.

"Sí."

"Could you get him, *por favor*?" The secretary lit another cigarette while she waited.

"*Chee-ye*?" said the ambassador, moments later.

"Salehi told me. Are you alright?"

"Of course I'm alright. I knew it was coming."

"What are you going to do? You're not going back to Tehran?"

"And face a firing squad like the Foreign Minister? No. I think I'll go to Washington for a while, see my daughter, see what's going on. Maybe the Americans have some plans for Iran. God knows, if they do they're not telling the embassy people here."

"What about me? What should I do?"

"Just wait until the new ambassador comes: he'll probably need a secretary who can speak three languages. Those mullahs can barely speak Farsi! But maybe you'll come to Washington later, when things are more settled; we can discuss it tonight. You certainly aren't thinking of going back to Tehran, are you?"

"No," replied the secretary, consciously steadying her voice. "I don't see myself in a chador. And actually, I don't think I can come over tonight. I'm not feeling very well."

"Don't be silly. Come over and I'll make you feel better."

"No, really. That time of the month." she lied. "Just happened."

"Oh, alright" said the ambassador after a moment of silence. "Listen, call the travel agent and see if you can get me on a flight to Washington for the day after tomorrow, or the day after that. I suppose I'll have to go through Miami?"

"Yes," replied the secretary. "I'm fairly certain."

"Take care of it, would you? And you can come over tomorrow night."

"*Baleh, ghorboun*." The secretary put the receiver down and picked up another cigarette. "Motherfucker," she muttered.

Salehi sat in the telex room, encoding a reply for Tehran. His concentration was broken by the loud ring of his phone. "*Baleh*?" he said with a start.

"Señor Shirazi to see you. Shall I show him to your office?"

"Yes, I'll be there in a m-minute." Salehi looked at his watch. It was already night in Tehran and the minister wouldn't see his telex until the morning anyway. He got up and walked back to his office. "*Agha-ye* Shirazi," he said as he stepped into the room. "Th-Thank you for coming."

"My pleasure," said Shirazi, standing up to shake Salehi's hand, who obliged and then sat down behind his desk.

"Mr. Shirazi, m-may I call you M-Mohammad?"

"Of course; please,"

"M-Mohammad Ali, we have a little p-problem here at the embassy. The ambassador is l-leaving and the F-Foreign M-Ministry wants you to p-protect the re-revolution's interests."

"Me? You're joking!"

"No, I'm n-not," said Salehi.

"They asked for me? I didn't even know there was going to be a revolution."

"Well, they d-didn't actually ask for you by n-name b-but there has to be someone r-revolutionary at the embassy."

"Then get a revolutionary."

"There's n-no one else in this c-country," pleaded Salehi. "P-Please; it's only until a n-new ambassador is ap-appointed."

"Am I getting paid?' asked Shirazi.

"I d-don't think s-so. B-But I c-can ask."

"What exactly would I have to do?" Shirazi's mind, usually at rest, was starting to work.

"N-Nothing, really," said Salehi. "I'll b-be here, and there's n-not much to do anyway."

"Where's the ambassador now?"

"At the R-Residence, I think. D-Do you want t-to speak t-to him?"

"Yes," said Shirazi, thinking. "You know, Salehi, I was once arrested by the SAVAK."

"R-Really?" Salehi picked up the phone and dialed the Residence.

"Yes," continued Shirazi. "Actually, I was not just arrested; I was beaten and tortured. For a week. No food, no water, and they kept my hands and feet bound the whole time." Salehi held up his hand to interrupt him and spoke into the receiver.

"M-Maria, is the ambassador in?"

"Sí."

"D-do you think I c-could speak with him?" Salehi glanced at Shirazi, who took the opportunity to continue his story.

"As I was saying, I was arrested by the SAVAK a number of times. It's a miracle I survived."

"M-My G-God yes!" said Salehi, holding the mouthpiece away. "I d-didn't know anyone could survive that long without w-water."

"I'm a very strong man," said Shirazi. "But Imam Hossein came to my rescue."

"Of course. The *Imam* s-saved you!"

"What?" The ambassador was on the line. "Have you gone mad, Salehi?"

"I'm s-sorry, s-sir, I wasn't speaking to you," said Salehi, holding his hand up again to signal Shirazi.

"Then what do you want?" asked the ambassador.

"S-Sir, I've got Mr. Shirazi here. F-for the re-revolutionary government's interests? He wants to s-speak with you, s-sir."

"What does he want?"

"I'm n-not sure, s-sir. Shall I p-put him on the l-line?"

"No, certainly not," said the ambassador. "I'm coming to the office to collect some things; tell him to wait for me."

"Yes, s-sir," said Salehi, and he hung up the phone. He took out his handkerchief and wiped his palms. "The ambassador is c-coming to the office," he said to Shirazi.

"When's he coming?" asked Shirazi. "I'm a busy man."

"It won't be l-long; a f-few m-minutes maybe. The Residence is r-right n-next door." Salehi paused for a moment. "Mohammad Ali," he said, "what d-do you d-do f-for a living? D-didn't you once tell me y-you are in import-export?"

"That's right, that's what I mainly do."

"What d-do y-you import and export?"

"This and that," replied Shirazi. He took out a pack of cigarettes from his pocket and offered one to Salehi.

"N-No thank you."

"These are real Winstons," said Shirazi, still holding the pack out to Salehi. "American Winstons, straight from America."

"I d-don't s-smoke," said Salehi. "B-But thanks." Shirazi shrugged his shoulders and lit one for himself.

"Anyway, as I was saying, the SAVAK never stopped harassing me. The fucking Shah deserves to die."

"Excuse me," said Salehi. "I have t-to s-send a t-telex to Tehran. C-Can I leave you here?"

"Sure," said Shirazi, blowing a long stream of smoke toward him. Salehi stood up and headed for the door. He opened it and paused, turning around to face Shirazi again.

"Then y-you'll w-work with us?" he asked.

"I suppose so," said Shirazi. "I'll do my duty. But find out how much I'll get paid. The embassy has a bank account here, right?"

"Yes," said Salehi. "But I'm n-not sure the g-government expects t-to pay you. I think they think y-you'd *w-want* t-to d-do this."

"Ask anyway."

Shirazi finished his cigarette and stood up. He wandered about the office, looking at the tourism posters on the wall and at the papers on Salehi's desk. Finding little of interest, he opened the door and walked down the hall to the ambassador's office. He stopped briefly at the secretary's desk to announce himself, "Mamad-Ali Shirazi." He then opened the ambassador's door.

"The ambassador's not in," said the secretary, standing up. "Can I help you?"

"No, I'll wait for him in here."

"I don't think he's coming in. Perhaps you should make an appointment."

"He's coming, and I'm with the embassy now. The *revolutionary* embassy."

"Oh," said the secretary. "But wait, you can't just go in!" she cried as Shirazi strolled into the ambassador's office.

"Thank you," said Shirazi, not turning around. "And get a photo of Imam Khomeini for your desk." He closed the door behind him.

"Fuck you too," muttered the secretary. "Fuck you and your *revolutionary* embassy."

At 3:00 p.m., the ambassador walked back into the Chancery building carrying a large briefcase. "*Chetori, khanoom jan*?" He asked as he reached his secretary's desk.

"He's in your office," she replied without looking up.

"Who? Salehi?"

"No, Shirazi," she said still not looking up. "The 'revolutionary.'"

"What's he doing in there?" said the ambassador, opening the door to his office. The secretary looked up at him and shrugged her shoulders. He stepped in and closed the door.

"*Salaam*," said Shirazi from behind the large leather-topped desk.

"*Salaam*," replied the ambassador. "Excuse me, do you mind?" He waited for Shirazi to get out of his chair. Shirazi took a long drag from his cigarette and slowly stood up.

"*Basheh*, have a seat," he said, and walked over to one of the armchairs. The ambassador put his briefcase on the floor and sat down in his chair.

"Well, what do you want?" he asked.

"Just wanted to ask a few questions," said Shirazi. "You know that I was tortured by SAVAK?"

"No," said the ambassador, "I didn't know. I'm very sorry for you, but I don't even know who you are."

"I'm Mamad-Ali Shirazi."

"Nice to meet you."

"Tell me, who's the SAVAK agent at the embassy?"

"I doubt very much we have one," said the ambassador, opening a drawer and taking out some papers. He looked through them and then put them in his briefcase. "You see that it can't be Salehi, and I'm the ambassador. And we're the only diplomats here. Besides, what would a SAVAK man do in this country?"

"Then you can't know how badly I was tortured. Six weeks in jail! No food or water for six weeks!"

"I wasn't aware a man could live for six weeks without water," said the ambassador matter-of-factly. "You must have been protected by *Allah*."

"Allah and the Imams — certainly. Has SAVAK been disbanded?"

"Indeed, it has," replied the ambassador. "And General Nassiri — its head, I presume you know — has been shot. Several times, I believe. Did you see the photos in the papers?"

"Yes, yes, I suppose I had. And what exactly do you do here?" asked Shirazi.

"Not much," said the ambassador, picking up the bottle of scotch again. "Do you want a drink?"

"Sure."

"Then get me that other glass from the coffee table." The ambassador poured himself a large shot and waited for Shirazi's glass. After he had filled it, he raised his own glass in the air. "*Be-salamati*!" he said.

"*Salamati*!" echoed Shirazi, draining his glass. The ambassador reached across his desk for the cigarette box. Shirazi leaned forward and offered his pack. "Those are stale," he said, "try these. American Winstons, straight from America."

"Thanks," said the ambassador, taking the proffered cigarette. "Not much happens here, Mamad-Ali," he said. "Iran has no vital interests here, so don't worry about a thing. The Shah thought that the more embassies and consulates we have around the world the more civilized we are. It was fine with me: little work and much play. Perfect for a long-divorced man like me." He pointed to the whiskey bottle. "Do you want another drink?"

"Sure," Shirazi held his glass out and the ambassador filled it to the brim.

"*Salamati*!"

"To the Revolution!" said Shirazi and took a large gulp.

"Mamad-Ali," said the ambassador. "You may want to be careful about drinking to an *Islamic* revolution."

"Actually, I don't drink," said Shirazi indignantly, quickly putting his glass down. "I was only being polite."

"Yes, of course. Thank you for drinking with me. May your sins be forgiven."

"When are you leaving?" asked Shirazi, pushing his glass away.

"In a couple of days," said the ambassador.

"Can I use your house then?"

"I don't see why not."

"Your office?"

"Work it out with Salehi. He's the Chargé d'Affaires now."

"Then he's in charge?"

"Mamad-Ali, it's a *revolution*, not a coup: no one knows who's in charge." He opened another drawer and looked through some more papers before throwing them in his briefcase. "Mamad-Ali," he said again, looking up at Shirazi, "Let me be honest with you. I don't care anymore." He stood up and picked up his briefcase. "If you have any questions, just ask Salehi."

"I have to go too," said Shirazi, pushing his glass even further away and standing up. "I'm a busy man." The ambassador walked to the door and opened it. He turned to Shirazi, who was standing right behind him.

"There is one thing you can do right away," he said. "Only if you want, of course."

"What's that?" asked Shirazi.

"You can take that picture of the Shah down, and replace it with whatever they send you." The ambassador pointed at the wall.

"*Plus* ça *change*," he sang and walked away.

THE APPRENTICE

J. D. DANIELS

There is nothing Satan likes better than telling himself he has powers equal to those of his creator, God; there is nothing a little boy likes better than telling himself he is the sexual equivalent of his big adult father, fit to be the consort of his own mother; and there is nothing an American likes better than telling himself he is more qualified to be president than that office's holder, which is why it is so grievous that we have elected such an incontinent, intemperate fool to our presidency. Satan is not God, and you are not your own father; but your competence as a mature adult almost certainly exceeds that of the current president of the United States.

The great psychoanalyst Janine Chasseguet-Smirgel writes:

> Lucifer is a perfect example of Hubris, of man's desire to discredit the power of the Father-Creator, and put himself in His place [...] The faulty identification with the father — the subject wanting to become God.

A foundational American myth, the American Revolution, is our refusal to obey our king. Traditional American authority derives from hatred of authority itself, from debasing and destroying existing authority. There is no surer path to political power in our country than for a candidate to proclaim that he is a rebel angel, not a politician. Unfortunately for him, once elected, he becomes a politician; and Americans, like willful children, cannot bear to be ruled.

You don't have to be religious, or to take psychoanalysis seriously, to see the analogy. Now is the most dangerous, most seductive moment of all. If you believe you would be a better head of the government than our president, you may be correct. Hubris and reality have aligned. The Satanic fantasy has become a fact.

There is nothing the apprentice likes better than telling himself he is the sorcerer. Many readers will recall an episode from the Disney film *Fantasia* in which Mickey Mouse believes he can outdo his master at wizardry. The enchanted brooms he uses to do his washing chores obey his command at first, but will not stop when the washing is finished.

As Goethe has it:

> And they run! Wet and wet
> in the hall and on the steps:
> What terrible waters!
> Lord and Master, hear my call!
> Oh, Master, come!
> Lord, the need is great!
> The spirits I have summoned
> will not depart.

But the sorcerer will not return: there is no sorcerer. There is only the foolish apprentice, who so wished to be greater than his master that he elected a still greater fool over himself, to rule him. He will drown.

WHAT GERSHOM SCHOLEM AND HANNAH ARENDT CAN TEACH US ABOUT EVIL TODAY

GEORGE PROCHNIK

WHEN GERSHOM SCHOLEM, the humanist scholar of Jewish mysticism, first met the philosopher Hannah Arendt in the 1930s he was bowled over by her intelligence and delighted by her character. To Walter Benjamin, he wrote excitedly that Arendt was rumored to have been Martin Heidegger's most brilliant student. To another friend, he described Arendt as "a wonderful woman and an extraordinary Zionist." He was moved by her work as director of the Paris office of Youth Aliyah, which helped refugee Jewish children from all over Europe get to Palestine. The fact that Benjamin — Scholem's intellectual idol, the man he would later say taught him what "thinking really means" through his own "living example" — came to value Arendt's writing and conversation imbued her with a special aura of intellectual gravitas.

The three spent time together in Paris in 1938 when Scholem was en route from Jerusalem to the United States to deliver the lectures that would become his breakthrough work of scholarship, *Major Trends in Jewish Mysticism*. Scholem, then 41 years old, and Arendt, nine years his junior, held long conversations about Benjamin's genius, in which Scholem took note approvingly of her aversion to the historical materialists Benjamin associated with at Max Horkheimer's Institute for Social Research. The pair of them, Scholem resolved, were kindred Jewish spirits with a metaphysical bent. They understood the transcendent implications of Benjamin's identification of critics with alchemists, probing the enigma of "the truth whose living flame goes on burning over the heavy logs of the past and the light ashes of life gone by."

Arendt seemed to reciprocate Scholem's expansive admiration. In the review she eventually published of his *Major Trends*, she declared that Scholem had not only recuperated Jewish mysticism as an essential strand in the larger tradition, but had actually transformed "the whole picture of Jewish history." The most revolutionary element in Scholem's exposition was his account of how both the Kabbalah's teachings about individual responsibility for the universe, and the public activities that grew out of its mystical doctrines, turned the Jew from a passive victim to an agent with free will able to become "a protagonist in the drama of the World." Thus, in Scholem's interpretation, Sabbatai Sevi, the Jewish false messiah, who sparked a wildly disruptive international movement in the 17th century, was not just a destructive lunatic, but also the unwitting inspiration for a new model of Jewish political activity. The novel lines of emancipatory speculation unleashed by this mystical redeemer had ramifications far beyond the folds of the religion, Arendt observed. Scholem's book clarified "for the first time the role played by the Jews in the formation of modern man." The catastrophe of Sabbatai Sevi, "after closing one book of Jewish history, becomes the cradle of a new era," Arendt concluded.

Scholem was thrilled with Arendt's assessment of his work's significance, calling her review one of just two "intelligent criticisms" the book had received. But the questions of human agency and of hapless victimhood raised by his study — questions of good, evil, and historical responsibility toward the dead and the future — would resurface in the controversy that ensued 15 years later over Arendt's book about Adolf Eichmann's trial in Jerusalem. And on this latter occasion, the split in their positions on these topics was so bitter that it destroyed their friendship. Ultimately, Scholem and Arendt were wrestling with the problem of how a person of conscience should address the unconscionable. The argument between them over the mindset of the evildoer continues to be relevant as we struggle to make sense of — and resist — the executors of cruel policy in our own time.

Hannah Arendt's coverage of Eichmann's 1961 trial began as a series of articles for *The New Yorker*, and was subsequently published in book form with the provocative subtitle, "A Report on the Banality of Evil." For some readers, the work was a paragon of unsentimental truth-telling that revealed how ordinary people could commit atrocities after surrendering their individuality to the faceless bureaucratic mechanisms that typified modernity. But the work has also been vehemently critiqued for allegedly downplaying the enormity of Eichmann's monstrousness (the terms banality and genocide don't comfortably mesh) and for the prominent attention Arendt gave to Jewish complicity in the Nazi program through — most glaringly — the work of Jewish Councils in overseeing or otherwise abetting the selection process for deportation to the concentration camps.

The shocked outrage Scholem felt on reading this work by a friend whom he'd formerly described as "one of the best minds" to flee Europe shared features with the larger mainstream Jewish intellectual repudiation of Arendt's project. But there was another dimension to Scholem's critique that has received less notice, yet which merits consideration in our current predicament. This particular aspect may also be indebted to moral perspectives Scholem absorbed from the Kabbalah for which, he once wrote, "the metaphysical cause of evil is seen in an act which transforms the category of judgement into an absolute."

The first letter Scholem wrote Arendt after reading her book — the initial broadside in an exchange that was ultimately made public — began with a number of concessions to Arendt's position on the Jewish role in facilitating the operation of the Holocaust. Having spent the past 50 years occupying himself with Jewish history, Scholem declares, he is well aware of the abysses in this narrative: "a demonic decay in the midst of life, insecurity in the face of this world [...] and a weakness that is perpetually confounded and mingled with debasement and with lust for power." It's invariable, he asserts, that in times of catastrophe these tendencies come to the fore. The question that the young were asking in Israel of how all those millions could have allowed themselves to be killed was valid, he allowed. Arendt was right to want people to reflect on such matters. What he cannot countenance is the idea that such a harrowing dilemma could be resolved with a snappy formula. What is unbearable to him, Scholem writes, is the "*malicious* tone" Arendt has adopted to discuss matters of such profundity. It is Arendt's "light-hearted style," the note of "English flippancy" she has favored over that of pity for Eichmann's victims — just as she has preferred snarkily caricaturing Eichmann himself to seriously analyzing his character — that repulses Scholem.

Nestled inside Arendt and Scholem's discussion of the nature of evil is a controversy over language. Scholem implies that the cool register of urbane wit Arendt employs not only fails to capture the essence of the event she is witnessing, but actually contributes to the project of dehumanization that Eichmann helped actualize. She loses sight of her subject in the sparkling exercise of her own cleverness. Ironically, in accusing Arendt of practicing facile mockery at the expense of real engagement with the events in Jerusalem, Scholem is charging Arendt with the flipside version of the crime she pins on Eichmann himself: thoughtlessness. Only in Arendt's case it is an excess of linguistic dexterity that fouls up her thinking rather than the deficit she perceives in Eichmann.

Arendt's diagnosis of Eichmann's banality was not intended to minimize the harm he inflicted, as she attempted repeatedly to make clear in response to attacks against her work, but to underscore his mediocrity. In Arendt's view, Eichmann's astonishing superficiality, on display throughout his trial, could be understood as even more ominous than the character of some classic satanic figure since it represented an easily communicable strain of wickedness. Eichmann's banality underscored the susceptibility of unremarkable men and women to becoming collaborators in spectacular crimes under pressure of the right kind of leadership and within the self-contained moral universe of bureaucratic systems that enabled perpetrators to shuck off their sense of personal responsibility. As Arendt, wrote Scholem, having watched Eichmann in action she had ceased to believe in the idea of "radical evil" that had been part of her philosophical lexicon in her earlier work on totalitarianism. Evil, she now proposed, had no depth, "and therefore has nothing demonic about it. Evil can lay waste the entire world, like a fungus growing rampant on the surface."

Face to face with the phenomenon of Eichmann in Jerusalem, Arendt became convinced that his actions betrayed not a monstrous personality, but a total inability to think for himself. And her principal evidence for Eichmann's cognitive ineptitude was his spluttering language. Over and over, Arendt marvels at the stupendous infelicity of Eichmann's word choices and his reliance on stock phrases. "Dimly aware of a defect that must have plagued him even in school — it amounted to a mild case of aphasia — he apologized, saying, 'Officialese [*Amtssprache*] is my only language,'" Arendt recounts at one point. However, she continues, "officialese became his language because he was genuinely incapable of uttering a single sentence that was not a cliché." The ghastly incoherence of Eichmann's hackneyed speech reflected the unoriginality of his mind, a thought process fatally clogged with grandiose, vacuous slogans.

Arendt later confessed herself to be continually fighting back laughter while she sat in the stands listening to him. In her book, she noted that the taped police examination of Eichmann offered a veritable gold mine to the psychologist "provided he is wise enough to understand that the horrible can be not only ludicrous but outright funny." Some of this comedy, she went on, couldn't be captured in English, however, since "it lies in Eichmann's heroic fight with the German language, which invariably defeats him."

Arendt's portrait of Eichmann has been challenged repeatedly over the years. But the recent biography by Bettina Stangneth, *Eichmann Before Jerusalem: The Unexamined Life of a Mass Murderer*, has been seized on by Arendt's critics as the most devastating rebuttal to her argument. Drawing on an enormous trove of personal and official documents that Arendt did not have access to, Stangneth reveals Eichmann to have been a far stronger character than the mindless functionary Arendt depicted.

Yet while it's true that Eichmann's anti-Semitism and overall devotion to the National Socialist party come through more forcefully in Stangneth's work than in Arendt's book, one does not necessarily come away from *Eichmann Before Jerusalem* feeling that he has been exposed as a fanatic, frothing ideologue. Eichmann was an exemplary Nazi from the start of the movement until the end, but Arendt never suggests otherwise. What does change dramatically is the impression of Eichmann's self-importance. He is a monster of self-regard and self-interest, savagely expedient in advancing his fortunes, with a fanatical hunger to be recognized as a great historical figure coupled to an instinct for personal survival at all costs. One of the most striking images in the book is of Eichmann steadfastly compiling a colossal file of press cuttings about himself which he continued to work on up until the final months of the war. Even when the coverage was negative, the sight of his name in print proved an irresistible intoxicant to Eichmann. "Nobody else was such a household name in Jewish political life at home and abroad in Europe as little old me," he later boasted to one friendly interviewer.

What Arendt failed to register in Jerusalem was that the stumbling, jargon-y, nonsensical *joke* of Eichmann's speech was intensely effective at maximizing his wiggle room before the law. By being as unclear as possible, Eichmann cast not just his own testimony but the facts themselves into a soupy haze of ambiguity. Moreover, it's plain that by doggedly mangling the language Eichmann struck the Achilles' Heel of high intellectuals like Arendt, triggering an urge to snicker even when the subject under discussion was the near annihilation of European Jewry. A buffoon who doesn't even have the mental wherewithal to defend himself except in comically inarticulate banalities is not someone an intelligent person with a liberal bias readily sends off to the gallows. What Arendt missed above all was the possibility that mediocrity could be performed, and that the man under trial for his life might be a versatile shape-shifter, constantly adjusting his clown act to make his character appear — not innocent of the acts he was accused of — but potentially exculpable by virtue of inanity.

¤

Scholem's fascination with Kabbalah was born in part out of frustration with the 19th-century advocates of so-called rational Judaism, the proto-progressive Jewish philosophers who wanted to purge the religion of all but its most universally acceptable, benign, anodyne features. "Jewish philosophy paid a heavy price for its disdain of the primitive levels of human life," he wrote. It effectively became out of touch with the experience of ordinary men and women. To the Kabbalists, on the other hand, evil was always "one of the most pressing problems," Scholem wrote, and they were "continuously occupied with attempts to solve it." In so doing, they spoke to the people's terrors and hopes, giving cosmic significance to both historical trauma and the anguish of everyday life.

One way of thinking about Scholem's objection to Arendt's "slogan" (as he called it) regarding evil's banality was that it did not connect to people's lived experience of suffering, which called out for empathy not aperçus. In the complex theological architecture of Kabbalah, evil is a quality originating within the Divine itself, which has somehow become isolated from tempering attributes. On the simplest level, the Divine aspects of judgment and wrath become detached from mercy and love, spawning the evil forces that plague humanity.

Scholem accuses Arendt of having let her sense of critical judgment run away with her to such an extent that she becomes numb to the human reality at issue. Of the decisions made by the leaders of the Jewish Councils, he acknowledges that, as is true of humanity in general, some were indubitably villains while others were saints. What's incontestable, he avows is that they were compelled to make decisions under conditions of such unique, immeasurable horror that their circumstances cannot be reconstructed. He himself, Scholem declares, is incapable of judging these representatives of Jewish communities. For a tragedy of such magnitude, sheer compassion for the collective — love — must guide the intellectual response at every step.

Scholem doesn't ask Adorno's question as to whether poetry is possible after the Holocaust, but he does suggest that in reporting on the Holocaust snide journalism may only further obscure the truth.

¤

Were he to have viewed today's battlegrounds, physical and moral, I suspect Scholem would have felt that expressing a solemn, absolute solidarity with those suffering the abuse of power constituted a more substantial form of resistance than even the most scintillating satiric takedown of those in command. We get pleasure from the fool, and turning agents of cruelty into fools risks making them a source of amusement whose risibility we secretly, guiltily itch to keep watching. The solidification of the status quo as entertainment (however dark) becomes its own form of normalization. (I remember hearing someone, an erstwhile Clinton supporter, crowing in the immediate aftermath of the elections, "I just can't wait to see Melania on *Saturday Night Live*.")

Scholem's final objection to Arendt's famous phrase returns to the quandary of Eichmann's character. What was really going on in his head when he supervised the transportation of hundreds of thousands of people to the extermination camps? If Hitler's project originated in a politics of wrath, what enabled its ongoing implementation by all those executors among whom Eichmann's name looms so large?

In Arendt's view, the problem with Eichmann's thinking boils down to the fact that he is not thinking very much — not nearly enough. If he had been taught to think properly, he would necessarily have developed a moral intelligence she indicates. Scholem situated the problem elsewhere. Rather than focusing on Eichmann's thought process, Scholem concentrates on his feelings — Eichmann's passions. Thus, Scholem does not discount the notion of the "banality of evil" because Eichmann and the other Nazi henchman are zealous anti-Semites, or raging believers in any larger ideology. What Scholem singles out as the flaw in Arendt's phrase is that it fails to recognize the sheer *pleasure* involved in being a successful Nazi. Scholem would never have discounted the idea that the Nazi bureaucracy facilitated the movement's genocidal mission. But he couldn't accept that the bureaucracy was managed by homogenous, robotic drones fulfilling the will of the master. The operators of was bureaucratic machines can still themselves be vainglorious individuals fueled by low appetites. "I don't picture Eichmann, as he marched around in his SS uniform and relished how everyone shivered in fear before him, as the banal gentleman you now want to persuade us he was, ironically or not," Scholem wrote Arendt.

The more complete portrait of Eichmann that has emerged in recent years validates Scholem's impression. From the descriptions and interviews of Nazi functionaries he himself has read, Scholem reports, it appears, "The gentlemen enjoyed their evil, so long as there was something to enjoy. One behaves differently after the party's over, of course."

The enjoyment Scholem refers to is not simple sadism, but the thrill of experiencing a wild inflation of personal power — power over others, power to do as one privately wishes quite apart from any larger, theoretical ideology. What Scholem identifies in Eichmann is the excitement of feeling oneself to be a god.

There are plenty of directions we can turn our eyes today to test the respective theses of Arendt and Scholem about the mentality of those figures crafting policies that cause suffering to the innocent and harm to the planet. Are we seeing conformist functionaries mindlessly carrying out their nefarious duties? Or are we watching numbers of highly self-motivated individuals eagerly, sometimes even gleefully indulging an unconscionable greed for power in all its earthly forms? In Arendt's schema, given enough basic intelligence, the person who doesn't know how to think can be taught to do so. But the problem presented by someone in a self-centered passion is different. The person who thinks himself a God has to be removed from power before contradicting their fantasy becomes a capital offense.

A MAN WALKS IN AND REMOVES HIS HAT

LINA MARÍA FERREIRA CABEZA-VANEGAS

"You know," Yaneth says, "I saw the devil once." Yaneth is my grandmother's nurse, and she says this as she wipes my grandmother's chin with a napkin.

I'm sitting across from them, at the kitchen table in my grandmother's Bogotá apartment. Right where I would sit after birthdays and Sunday dinners listening to my grandmother tell me about all the ghosts that used to haunt her, and every demon that would — she promised — someday devour me.

I pause, "Do you mean the actual devil?"

My grandmother doesn't tell me stories anymore, doesn't speak to me, doesn't speak to anyone but Yaneth. *Oh but when we are alone, you should see it, Lina! How she goes on and on, isn't that true Doña Josefina?* I've never seen it, and doubt I ever will. It's difficult to picture this silent woman alone in a room with Yaneth — lively, friendly, arms waving, head thrown back — *carcajadas, risas y sonrisas*. I struggle to remember my grandmother laughing at all as I stare at her, slumped in a chair with a spine like a melting candle and eyes that skip shallowly over every object in view like pebbles across a black lake. *Oh, how she tells me stories, don't you Doña Josefina?*

"The very one." Yaneth says, "I saw the devil." While she feeds my grandmother beige slop and the metal spoon makes a plastic thud when it crashes against her dentures. "*El mismísimo diablo.*" My grandmother opens and closes her mouth like a bird in an abandoned nest.

"Really?" I straighten my back and lean in close.

My grandmother's maid, Kelly, emerges from the kitchen, beating something in a plastic bowl. "You know, the devil used to appear a lot more often, before."

Yaneth nods, "Oh yeah, back when. Real often."

Both Kelly and Yaneth are from the more rural and tropical parts of Colombia, Mompox and Chiriguaná respectively, and it goes without saying that I stand at a great disadvantage in most things magical, being from the temperate-weather Andean capital. I don't know what it is like being from a place where the heat rises from the earth and descends from the sky, and crushes everything in between and the devil still bothers to shows up every so often. "At least," Kelly says, "He used to."

"Like when?" I tap a granadilla fruit on the table cracking its thin-skull orange shell.

"Like," Yaneth feeds my grandmother another spoonful, "Few years back, my mom's friend's friend, she saw him."

"Wait. What?" I expected centuries, many decades at least.

Yaneth barely acknowledges my confusion and carries on with her story. "My mother's friend's friend, she saw him and told her how it happened." Yaneth turns for a moment, to remind my grandmother to swallow, *Ahí, mamá, traga, traga. Así sí.* "He was a nightmare, this terrible-terrible boy."

"Like … how terrible?" I ask while Kelly lingers in the doorframe, beating and nodding, "*Mmm-hmm. Mmm-hm,*" like she's seen the devil too.

"This boy, he used to throw these tantrums and yell and scream. Terrible boy. He hit his own mother even!" My grandmother hangs on Yaneth's every word, though I doubt she can understand much of it anymore. "But his mother, she was good, forgiving. A saint. So one day," Yaneth takes a breath, "she brings out his dinner — like always — a humble meal, and she sets it down right in front of him."

"Uh-huh." I say, peeling the orange shell from around the white-felt inner skin.

"And you know what he does?" Yaneth swallows saliva and opens her mouth to remind my grandmother how it's done. "This boy, he picks up the plate, and he throws it!"

"He didn't!" I say, "Did he?" I imagine myself as a child throwing a plate at my formidable Colombian mother, and I remember the swing, snap, and sting of her leather shoe striking my skin.

"The gall." I say.

"Yes," Yaneth agrees. "He was a terrible boy. Smashes it all to bits against the wall."

"No."

"Yes."

"Then what?"

"Well then comes a knock at the door."

"Right away?"

"*Right* away."

"Do they answer?"

"No."

"No?"

"No." Yaneth raises her eyebrows and turns her head, "Not *they* … he. The boy opens the door."

"Oh … I see."

Kelly is frying sweet plantain for lunch, but manages to emerge just at the right moments to punctuate the story with a nod or a sigh, as if to say, *Yeah, that sounds right.*

"Wait, wait, wait…" I say pulling out a pen and a few napkins from the dispenser.

A tall man.

"In a suit."

A tall man in a suit. With fangs, and horns, and skin like melting wax.

"No."

"No?"

"Just a suit. And he's handsome, and dark skinned too."

I look at Yaneth skeptically, "Are you sure?" I'm looking at her dark, freckled complexion and wonder if she's not just making devils in her own image.

She raises an eyebrow, "Yes. Also, he's handsome. Did you already write that part down?"

The terrible boy opens the door and finds a man in a suit. He is dark skinned and handsome. The man does not wait to be invited in, he simply walks in, and removes his hat.

"No, no, Lina." Yaneth scoffs. "Are you crazy? The devil does not wear a hat!"

I scratch out the sentence and start again.

He walks in and wipes his forehead with a white handkerchief.

"Yes," Yaneth agrees. "It's very hot. The handkerchief would make sense."

He approaches the boy and surveys the damage. Lentils and rice drip down from the wall and onto the shattered porcelain on the floor. He takes a deep breath and says, "Boy, please open your mouth." And the terrible boy does as he is told.

"Wait," I interrupt. "Really? Just like that? No questions?" I grab more napkins from the dispenser.

"Of course!" Yaneth says motioning with the spoon my grandmother follows like a baited hook. "It's the devil."

So, because this was the devil — and that is more than reason enough — the boy opens his mouth.

"But are you sure?" I insist. "Because, I think … If it were me, I might resist. At least a little."

"Well," Yaneth taps her chin. "Maybe, a little," she concedes.

But no one is ever willingly dragged to hell so the terrible boy snaps his mouth shut again and yells at the man in the suit, "No! I won't. And who are you to make me?" But the devil does not respond. The devil does not have to. He glows white-blue-black, the flickering of cold flames, and with a "tsk" of his tongue the boy's jaw drops, and he stands there wide-mouthed. Then the man reaches inside.

"Wait." I have ripped the napkin with my pen. "Into the boy's mouth?"

"Yes."

"Why?"

The boy's jaws are locked in place, pried open with invisible jacks as the man slides his hand inside. Like plumbers reach into clogged gutters, like magicians reach into hats. No rush at all as he digs his fingernails into the boy's tongue.

"I'm not sure about the fingernails." Yaneth says.

"Why not?"

"*Mi mamá*," she crosses herself in memory of her dead mother, "She never mentioned anything about fingernails."

"But, it's the devil, doesn't it seem right? Shouldn't he have long fingernails?"

"Hm…" Yaneth twists her mouth, wants to give this to me, but, "this is a true story," she says.

"Of course," I nod emphatically, "But tongues are slippery. That's true too, right?" I wait for her to consider my point, "Even if the nails aren't long he must have them, and squeeze hard enough, they'll break the skin. Right? And besides, how else would one get a grip?"

"Well…" She exhales, "I guess, that *is* true." She looks up at the ceiling giving it one final go over before nodding. "Yes, alright. Fingernails then."

> *The man can smell the boy's breath as he pushes him against the wall. He presses one hand against the boy's forehead to keep the head in place while he digs sharp finger tips into a pink tongue and begins to pull. He yanks, hard. Once, twice, thrice. Like he is trying to start a rusted lawnmower. Once, twice, thrice. Until little membranes start to give like the white roots of sprawling weeds, and nerves begin to send screaming pulses up the young man's spine. The boy tries to scream but it is a difficult thing to do with a man rhythmically tugging on his tongue. Once, twice, thrice. But he is in a trance, he does not yell, he does not resist, he does not move, he allows the rhythmic motion of the tall man's tugging. Once, twice, thrice. Again. Again. Repeat. It is as if the boy has already been tugged out of himself and is only able to watch the scene, from a little distance with the sound turned all the way down. He can only hear the sound of a fly crashing against a windowpane, lentils dripping from the wall, the fabric of the man's coat stretching around the seams. But then, also, the fizzing taste of rust.*
>
> *The boy swallows blood and suddenly, comes back into himself and he begins to squirm and struggle. He kicks the man in the ankle, kicks him in the shins. He reaches up, tries to scratch out the man's eyes, and — for a moment — he feels the man's grip loosen. Only a moment. Because it is just the shifting of forces. The man swats the boy's hands away, kicks his legs out from under him. He grabs the half-torn tongue like a fistful of hair …*

"But what about the mother?" I look up at Yaneth.
"What about her?" Yaneth wipes my grandmother's chin with the metal spoon.
"Where is she while all this is happening?"
"Well…" Yaneth motions with her head to a corner in the room. "Over there," and I look as if I might actually see a woman standing there.
"What do you mean?" I ask.
"Well, what do you mean?"
"Wouldn't she…" I'm not sure how to phrase it, "Intervene?"

> *The boy can barely scream, he gags, and gargles and chokes on his own blood. But this is enough for a mother. She feels the devil's hand as if it were inside her own mouth and around her own throat.*
>
> *So she shakes off whatever power has been holding her back and she throws herself at the man in the suit. She wraps her arms around his neck like a noose and yells at her son, "Go! Go-go-go!"*

"Yes," Yaneth concedes, "that sounds right," patting my grandmother on the forearm. "Mothers are very forgiving." I remember the time my younger sister split her bottom lip against the metal corner of a full-force swinging rusty jungle gym. It was a lip like an open book, pages ripped

KENYATTA A.C HINKLE, *THE EVANESCED #139*, 2016, INDIA INK ON RECYCLED ACID FREE PAPER, 9 X 12 INCHES / COURTESY OF THE ARTIST

apart, a vertical line made into two horizontal ones and an endless well of red in the middle. I remember my mother pushing down crowds and kicking moving cars until she got my sister to the hospital. Like how, one day, my grandmother saved me from my mother and her leather shoe insert after I'd done something particularly egregious. "If you hit this child," she said to my mother, "I will pull down your pants and beat you right back." It is one of my favorite memories of her. A frail body, even then, standing between the canon and the fodder before she even knew what I'd done. As Yaneth brushes my grandmother's hair behind her ear I also recall the time that, from her wheelchair, she tried to beat Yaneth with her cane.

> *It is only a moment. A few seconds, no more. But a few seconds are enough for the young man to kick his way out from under the man in the suit and run to the door. He is going to leave the room. He is going to run outside, into the bushes, down the river, and out of town. He is going to disappear and he is going to buy stationary in a corner shop in Madrid, in Buenos Aires, in Bogotá. And he is going to write his mother a letter from a far-off city where the devil does not appear so often. An apology on pink stationary with little white flowers on the corners, like the ones on his mother's favorite china, the one he broke against the wall all those years back. That's what the boy — because really he still only just a boy — tells himself, between one moment and the next. But somewhere in the mesh of white nylon ligaments and red yarn nerves he already knows that he will never leave this room again.*
>
> *He hears whispers the instant he places his hand on the doorknob. A cold, burning, solid sound. Something mercurial and acidic that flows and fills, and then congeals between the spaces of his ear canals and the lock on the door. He feels the sound like squirming pus and swelling eggs in his inner ear, and he screams. He clutches his ears and despite the crimson sound pulsing behind his eyes he still tries to turn the knob. But, of course, there's no use. He tries to pull and then to push, and then he bangs his fists on the wood as if someone were waiting for him on the other side. Since the knob won't turn, the boy finally does. The man stands perfectly still and perfectly composed in the middle of the room as a fly hits the glass one last time and collapses on the windowsill.*
>
> *There are no stains on the man's suit, no scrapes where he has been struck, no prints where he has been kicked, and no blood on his hands at all, so the boy begins to understand. This is not the devil of contracts and compromises, this is the devil of gavels and scales. His pockets are full of pulled teeth and plucked eyes, and what a mother is willing to forgive has no bearing on the task at hand. The devil tosses the woman across the room and she lands, unconscious, on top of shards of broken china. The man does not take his eyes off of the boy; he seems immobile and frozen in place, like he's always been there, like the jungle, always gnawing at the edges of the cities of men. Only of course he must have moved, he must have, because he was there, just right there and then here, now, with his hand around the boy's throat and tossing him to the ground. Then the man in the suit puts a foot on the boy's neck, and a hand insides his mouth and he pulls out the tongue like a sword from a stone.*

My handwriting has devolved into feral scratches while I try to catch up, and Yaneth gently wipes my grandmother's mouth with a clean napkin, calling her "*mami*" and "*mamá*," looking at her with more tenderness than I've ever mustered for anything on this earth. And I wonder if Yaneth knows that my grandmother would never have allowed this before her mind began to slip. "*They never know their place, these people,*" she used to say, "*always trying to 'ingualarcele a uno.' Sit at the table with you, as if they were anything like you, same as you. The gall!*" I feel a tightness in my chest.

"That's it, what must have happened."

I look up at her, "Then what?"

"Then *what* what?"

"Then … the end?"

Yaneth pauses, tilts her head back, looking at the ceiling like people glance at dictionaries and tarot decks. "*History!*" My grandmother used to correct me, *"Not stories, Lina. History is what I tell you."*

"He pulls," Yaneth clarifies, "until the boy is dead."

"The boy is dead."

"Yes. Of course, Lina, what did you think?"

"And then?"

"He leaves."

I remember standing in hallways and behind doors as a child, secretly listening to adults and news anchors as they named and counted the ways the men in the jungle, in the mountains, and the back alleys, might cut up a body. The one where the penis was stuck inside the mouth, the testicles inside the mouth, the head tucked like a baby in the wrapped arms of a headless torso, the belly hollowed out like a vase and severed limbs stuck inside it like wilting flowers; the one where the tongue is slipped through a slit in the neck like a very short tie. This one for the snitch, this one for the traitor, this one for the liberal, this one for the copper. This one, and this one, and this one for the terrible man, terrible woman, terrible child. For the terribly unlucky and terribly helpless in those terrible times.

This was before I knew anything. Before I knew that the tongue is a circular muscle and not a long strip of wet leather sliding down a constricting throat. Knew that it would take quite a bit of practice, patience, and knife, work to get the job done, get it to look right. Or how we get one *violencia* mixed up with another, get tangled in the mess of severed limbs laid out at our feet. It wasn't the cartels' innovation, like I first learned, but the *Chulavitas* during *La Violencia* of the '40s and '50s that in defense of their land and their party first reimagined the body like a set of spare parts to reassemble into grotesque threats and monstrous metaphors of an alienated nation.

I rest my face in my hands and think how my grandmother was barely 18 when *La Violencia* started, already two years into a decade of savage rural massacres and mutilations; then barely 20 when she married an air force pilot at the beginning of what would become a five decade civil conflict; and barely 32 when that pilot, fighting what would become one of the major guerilla groups in that conflict, fell to earth strapped to a faulty parachute. Dominoes, and bread crumbs, and chain-smoker wars — one lighting the next, and the next, and the next. I feel my face beneath my fingers and want to poke them through my skin like pencils into a ripe plum. "I thought … I don't know. That it was just a tongue. That he might live after all."

"He doesn't."

"No. Of course not."

"It's the devil, Lina."

"Yes, I know." I write "until dead" on my napkin, and retrace the words until they are bold.

"And then?" I ask, "The end?"

"Yes."

Kelly leans on the doorframe and makes a sort of *tsking* sound with her mouth. "See?" She exchanges glances with Yaneth once more. "He used to appear more often, *antes que ahora*." This, in the same tone people use when talking about global warming and violence on television. "It's a real shame."

I start brushing crumbs, pieces of granadilla shell and scrap pieces of torn napkin off the edge of the table and into my hand, but Kelly immediately rushes over, nudges my hand out of the way, and catches the trash in her own palm. This wordless motion turns my stomach.

"But, what do you mean, Kelly," I say, using slang and the informal *you* to try to counter history, social class, and this sinking feeling in my stomach.

"What do *you* mean, what do *I* mean?"

She's told me how much she hates the rain of the capital, the cold nights, the cold people. How much she missed her hometown, her family, and how the heat rises and falls and crushes everything in between. Then she sighs again and repeats that it's just such a shame the devil doesn't come around as often as he used to.

"Why?" I insist, "Why would you want him back? He's the devil."

Kelly pops back out holding a jar and she and Yaneth exchange glances, reminding me how out of the loop I really am. I stare at my grandmother as she sucks on her dentures and stares blankly, and I wonder if they know that in this one thing she isn't one of mine, but one of theirs.

"Back when," Yaneth says, "He'd show up and put things right." She takes a deep breath and seems suddenly exhausted as she exhales, "Put people in their place."

"Sometimes," Kelly speaks slowly, formally, and deferentially as if there is some old and unspoken debt between us, "You just wish he'd come back and do what he used to."

Kelly is small, skin the color of milk molasses, about an inch shorter than me, and about six months younger. She has a little boy, a husband who sometimes finds work in construction sites, and this large extended family that waits with bated breath for her to return for carnivals and bull runs.

"You see all these people. They do all these things. They do what they like, take what they want. And in broad daylight too. Like it's nothing, and we are no one and it's all actually true now. It doesn't matter what they do to us because we don't matter enough, because nothing happens when they take and do what they do, and no one comes when it happens. And that's how it is," she looks at me, "They made it true." *Not stories, Lina, histories.* She sighs like she has the whole weight of mountain ranges and civil wars bearing down on her shoulders, and I imagine arms and legs bursting out of hollow-pumpkin stomachs. Then Kelly meets my eyes. "We're nothing to them," she says, "And their opinion is all that matters, so that's what we are now." *Nada.* She looks at me as if I'm supposed to know what to say next, as if we weren't the same age, lived in the same country, through the same history. But then, of course we haven't. I am my grandmother's granddaughter, I am pale and when I was given the chance to leave, I did.

Yaneth wipes drool from my grandmother's blank face. "I don't know," says Kelly. "I wonder if there's going to be something like a second flood, or something."

"A reckoning." I say.

"Yes," Kelly nods. "A reckoning, that's what."

Bogotá is a city of overflow canals, twice daily rain, mudslides, and aisles full of umbrellas; it's not so hard to imagine it underwater. To see my lifeless body amid nine million others as we float up slowly to the surface while carving knives and rifles sink to the bottom. It's not so hard. My grandmother — olive green eyes, skin that blisters in the sun, veins as full of blood-thinner as the blood of a mixed heritage she would never admit to. I try to shake the image of water rising around her — toothless, frail, and wordless.

"But Yaneth. You haven't told us yet about the time you saw the devil."

Yaneth's complexion is a more decided mix of races than Kelly's indigenous-European brand, and I stupidly wish that my own skin would show more of the complications of my own disparate heritage. Darker like my maternal aunt's skin or the burnt-sugar tan of my younger sister's skin after a day in the sun. But I burn like a fuse, like hot oil and red wax. My skin shows only one side of this history, and one fraction of all the factions in my veins. When my blisters peel off, I go back to being pink and pale and raw. My grandmother used to tell me, "Your skin is my skin. Good, soft, and white — like mine," with pursed lips and head held high. "After how you were born, what a relief." Every birthday without fail, "You were the ugliest baby I'd ever seen. Black! Purple-black! And for a moment we thought you'd never get normal."

I pull my sleeves down to my wrists. "Well, Lina, here it is then." Yaneth takes a deep breath and I start pulling out scraps of paper from my pockets and bag, until I find an empty envelope to scribble on. "There was this thing I used to say, to dare *him* to appear."

I'm shocked; I gasp. This is the woman who told me that one should always sleep with open scissors beneath one's pillow to scare off witches, *See how they make the sign of the cross when you open them? Oh! And also, remember to leave a mound of salt by the front door and needles on the windowsill. Lina, that's very important. Witches cannot help themselves*, and when they see a pile of needles or a mound of salt, they must count every spindle and every grain. *And that takes a long time, and then morning comes.* Light chases away shadows and witches, and I imagine a trail of needles and salt like breadcrumbs back to the devil's doorstep.

I just can't believe it.

"Yaneth, really?"

"Yes, and, Lina." She is speaking quickly, making my grandmother nervously sink further back into her chair, "You can write it all. Every bit I tell you, except the chant."

I hesitate, "But…"

"Lina," She stops me. "You can't." With the look of a woman handing over a lit match and a full gas can. "These words are powerful. You can't."

"Ok, but why would you even chant at all?"

My grandmother shakes gently and reaches for Yaneth's hand. "*Ay, ay.*" Yaneth shakes her head, "*Aish*. Well, I didn't quite think it would work. Did I?" She laughs, but it is tense laughter. This is not a story.

A girl walks through the country roads of Chiriguaná with her best friend. They leap into the air, they twirl around one another. The warnings to stay close to the road only push them further and further away.

My grandmother is getting restless. She fidgets and whimpers like a restless child; she was a frail, asthmatic little girl. Neither of her parents' favorite child and possibly, as a result, she grew into a hypochondriac and a storyteller.

Then the girl's best friend picks up a stick and taps the fence as they walk beside it, and she begin to sing a secret song to a barbwire beat.

My grandmother's tales were my first literature. I know them by heart. The one about the ghost soldier banging his ghost shoes against her airbase bedroom door. The one where, standing in a yellow shrub garden, she told her very young granddaughters that the homeless man across the street would probably drag them to hell one day. The one about the day when her husband's parachute failed to open and he fell full-force into the earth's. "I heard it," she said. From miles and miles away, it sounded like "a silver pen striking the tile floor." The spirits let her know, she told me, and my mother and aunts can still remember crawling on hands and knees that Sunday afternoon looking for a ghost pen while their father fell from the sky.

"Histories, Lina."

They've done this before. Twice as many times, at least, as the times they've been told not to. They hold hands and spin around like a flashing carnival ride, singing faster and faster with each turn.

Maybe she saw the devil too. Looked at a history book, sat in a classroom, stared out from the coast and back into the former colony, and concluded that the devil lived in the details of accent, place, heritage, social class, and color. She was grateful that her own skin did not show all of her. She practiced telling people she was from Bogotá, she practiced the flat-edged accent of cold, pale Bogotá. Forcing her mouth to drop the long coastal vowels, pick up the R's and hold down the L's.

Nothing is expected to happen. The girls don't actually expect it to work. "Little devil come and play. With your sisters made of clay. Devil listen, devil pray. Come and play, come and play." Though, of course, if there were absolutely no chance it would work, there would also be no point in playing.

My grandmother's whimpering intensifies as Yaneth attempts to imitate herself as a child, and through a slit in the door, I see Kelly making the sign of the cross again, and again, and again.

The girls spin faster and faster until the blood pools in the back of their heads and they see each other grow pale and flat-faced in their improvised centrifuge and finally one of them lets go. One watching the other fly off into a whirling blur and collapse on to the ground.

A half turn and a full stumble, the standing girl remains standing as if my divine grace. She stumbles, and tilts. She nearly falls into the barbwire fence but rights herself by grabbing a hold of the fence posts, then she closes her eyes and tries to catch her breath. Hears the pounding of blood in her ear and the wolf-huffing of her lungs. And after her heart has settled and she has caught her breath, the gasping sound remains. And even before she has opened her eyes she knows that it is not the wind she feels on her cheeks, nor her own breath she hears so loudly and so clearly. Then she opens her eyes and comes face to face with a massive black dog.

The Chulavitas were named after a single dirt path in Boyaca. Just one. A conservative leaning country road built on the edge of a once holy city of the Muisca Confederation of tribes where, I imagine, many little girls must have also ran up and down the weed paths. Must have sung songs and played games while the Spaniards marched up steep Andean paths, while African slaves formed independent Palenque settlements, while a liberal leader was murdered in Bogotá, while their parents sharpened their machetes to the sound of radios reporting how liberals were — that very second —tearing out the beating heart of their beloved country.

> *Red eyes. But not the color of stop lights and lipstick. Full, and deep, like bubbles of blood about to pop. It does not snarl, it does not move. A steady stream of saliva drips from its mouth and steam rises from its nostrils. The girl can smell its breath, can feel the dampness of it on her cheeks. "Yaneth, Yaneth, Yaneth." The dog says. "Yaneth, Yaneth." These words have power. In a low gravel growl, an almost human sound, repeating her name like an incantation.*

I wonder if those little girls saw the devil too. Sculpted out of the dead, and the dying, and worn down into the blisters of their own feet as they walked the length of fields and roads to work as maids and nurses in a capital still digging itself out of the rubble of riot, rage, and revolt.

> *So the girl turns around, and she runs.*

"Wait." I say, "Why?"

"What do you mean, 'Why'?" Yaneth asks patting my grandmother's hand.

"Well, you can't outrun the devil. Can you?"

Yaneth pauses and it seems to me like this is something she has never considered before. My grandmother looks up at her, helpless and confused. And I feel grateful for Yaneth and her loyalty, wherever it may spring from, because I love my grandmother though I know her faults, and I love my country too, though I also know that they are not few, those who have been crushed between its gears. "No," Yaneth says, "I guess you can't." Yaneth shrugs, "But, what else?"

> *The girl sprints without a plan. She looks over her shoulder only for a moment and only every so often because she doesn't need to look. She can hear the dog behind her — the panting and the snarling and the wet* gal-foop-gal-foop *of its jowls and cheeks flapping against teeth and gums with each stride. Then a dip in the field where grass has made it seem even and flat, her foot falls through it, she trips, she begins to fall. She sees her hands go up instinctively as the ground approaches, but her legs run right under her and propel her forward with the momentum. She recovers her balance and pushes hard against the ground as if it too might be allied with the devil, and then she looks over her shoulder, the dog is still hot at her heels. She suddenly sees her uncle jumping up and down trying to get her attention on a dirt road of her hometown.*

Yaneth lets go of my grandmother's forearm for a second to illustrate the motion and this upsets my grandmother greatly. She looks up at Yaneth and whispers sentences that I can't quite make out at first. She speaks between wheezes, thin and shrill like wind sliding through broken reeds. But Yaneth understands her perfectly. She lays her hands on hers and order is instantly restored — walls, meridians, gravity, and laws emerging from the darkness and lining the borders of my grandmother's new universe. "It's okay *Mamá*," Yaneth says to my grandmother, "in just a minute we'll go."

> *The girl's uncle is scrawling frantically on the dirt while she runs toward him. This would have likely struck her as odd had she not at that moment been possessed by the spirit of all the prey who ever tried to escape the snapping jaw of a predator, and failed.*

Yaneth stands up to get the wheelchair and my grandmother follows her with her eyes. She briefly loses Yaneth from sight and a thin layer of panic settles on her face. In my mind, she is forever sitting on the edge of an unfathomably uncomfortable Louis XVI replica sofa, two or three feet away from where she sits now, where the living room begins. She raises her hands showing me her palms and outstretched fingers, and then one by one she touches the tip of each digit with the index finger of the opposite hand. "One, two, three," she counts, "four, five, six, seven. That's what he'd tell me every night." She would remember her nights in an air force base in the middle of a jungle and a nascent civil war, watching her husband count invisible cows. "He'd sit me down and he'd show me his hand and say, 'That's how many we have now, Coca. That's how many I've bought you and wait for us back in Mompox for when this is all done.'" This is what she looked like when she spoke of the colonel and how alone he left her in this world: a constant muted panic that outlasted her long years of mourning.

Then Yaneth parks the wheelchair next to my grandmother's chair and sits back down.

> *The girl approaches the road. She sees it closing the distance as if it were moving toward her and not her toward it. She jumps over the fence and runs across the road and pictures her uncle walking to the window, across the room she shares with her siblings. He used to pile needles on the windowsill and explain witches' uncontrollable need to count every needle and every grain of salt. "Morning will find them," she hears him say, "And light will sweep them away." The girl opens her eyes and finally looks over her shoulder fearing the worst.*

"It was really very scary. *Aish* Lina!" Yaneth places her hand on her forehead and exhales, "If you had seen it. No-no-no-no-no." In the kitchen, I see Kelly shake her head, "Only to think about it and my little hairs stand up, look, see?" She offers me her forearm as proof.

> *But the worst hasn't happened. Her uncle has escaped the hell hound. He is a man who knows to leave salt on the windowsill and scissors beneath pillows, and he also knows to draw a cross in the devil's path.*
>
> "And?"
> "That was it."
> "That worked?"
> "Yes."
> "It disappeared?"
> "When I turned around, it was gone."

I watch Yaneth help my grandmother into her wheelchair, picture dawn sweeping memories away like witches and demons. I think of my grandmother as a child sitting quietly at the dining room table after her father had thrown a plate across the room. Puddles of food on the floor, mounds of broken porcelain strewn around, and a streak of red sauce across her cheek while the heat of her father's rage slipped out the window and the heat of a tropical city slipped right back inside.

I imagine her in front of a mirror practicing her new accent. It is a story she never told me, but I know it by heart: how she pulled on her own tongue and felt it tug back, as she tried desperately to correct the course of her own history. My eyes fall on my one saving grace — the pink-pale skin of my arms. I run a finger over the napkin incantation I must never share with anyone, and allow my pen to draw full circles on my skin.

SNAP AS REVOLUTIONARY TIME

SARA AHMED

A REVOLUTION CAN REFER to the forcible overthrow of an existing regime. It can refer to a dramatic change to existing circumstances brought about by something or by a combination of things. When a revolution has happened we are no longer where we were before. A revolution can seem sudden; what was is not. Yet the word evolves from revolve; to turn back or roll back. A revolution can mean the time it takes for an object to orbit around a center. These meanings of revolution seem to be in tension; fast forward, a break from before; going back; going around.

My task is to hold on to these tensions, not to resolve them. Snap is a way of holding on. Why snap? A snap is the sound something makes when it breaks. Something snaps because it is under pressure. A snap happens after the pressure has reached a certain point. You can hear the sound of snap, but it is hard to notice pressure unless you are under it. A snap can sound like the start of something. But a snap would only be the start of something because of what we do not notice: the pressure on something that can break something.

When we snap, it might be that we speak in a certain way; we might snap *at* someone, break a bond *with* someone. Even this kind of snap can take time to reach. You might be in a relationship with someone who is violent. Relationships that are hard to endure can be hard to leave. You might have been told by a person that you are beneath that person; that you are worth nothing, that you are nothing. But there can be a point, a breaking point, when you can no longer put up with what had previously been endured. Something snaps; you snap. It can seem sudden. A refusal can appear to come out of nowhere. But a refusal comes from somewhere. Perhaps the slow time of bearing can only be ended by a sudden movement. Or perhaps the movement only seems sudden because we do not witness the slower times of bearing. If snap breaks with what came before, snap comes out because of what came before; going back as coming forward. Maybe in snap something or somebody spins off their axis, a revolution as how you no longer revolve around somebody or something.

See how she spins; out of control.

Snap seems here firmly embedded within a situation; snap as interpersonal. How do we get from a situation to a revolution? For an individual, a snap, that moment when she does not take it anymore can be experienced as revolution; snap as how an existing order is overthrown. Snap: a moment with a history. A moment can be a movement. Snap might be already implicated in how movements come about. Consider the Stonewall riots. In an interview with Eric Marcus conducted in 1989, Sylvia Rivera describes what happened on that day. Sylvia Rivera as a trans woman of color tends not to be remembered in how those events are remembered. She describes how that day was a day like any other day for those who gathered at the bar; those used to living with police violence; those for whom it was violence as usual. Rivera says: "This is what we learned to live with at that time. We had to live with it." You learn to live with what makes it hard to live. You take it, knowing there will be more to take.

But something happens on that day. Something happens: you just don't take it anymore. "We had to live with it until that day. And then, I don't know if it was the customers or it was the police. It just [snaps fingers], everything clicked." The snapping of fingers, that sound, snap, snap, allows Rivera to convey the sensation of things falling into place, when suddenly, though it only seems sudden from the outside, really it took a long time, a collective comes out with a "no," a collective that is fragile, fabulous, full, and furious. She says: "Everybody just like, *Why the fuck are we doin' all this for?* Oh, it was so exciting. It was like, Wow, we're doing it. We're doing it. We're fucking their nerves."

We can hear the sound of snap in listening to Rivera. You can hear how a snap can be catchy, igniting a crowd, passing from one to another. We can hear how you can be picked up by other peoples' refusal. All those years of frustration, pain, all that is wearing, can come out, get out. It is electric, snap, snap; sizzle, so much comes out when you tip something over. To make snap part of how we tell the story of political movements is to show how exhaustion and rebellion can come from the same place. Attending to snap allows us to re-picture the revolutionary not as the upright agentic figure filled with capacity but as the one who is just plain exhausted. And yet, even when snap comes from sap, from being tired out, depleted, snap can reboot; snap can boost.

Snap that moment when the pressure has built up and tipped over, is revolting, a revolt against what we are asked to put up with. Snap here is not only about individual action, those moments when she does not take it anymore, when she reacts to what she has previously endured, though it includes those moments. A movement is necessary so a moment can happen, a moment when the violence comes out; spills out. A movement is necessary. Snap makes what is necessary possible.

DARK ON BOTH SIDES

KAVEH AKBAR

Dark on both sides.
Makes a window.
Into a mirror. A man.
Holds his palms out to gather.
Dew through the night. Uses it.
To wash before.
Dawn prayer. Only a god.
Can turn himself into.
A god.
The earth buckles.
Almond trees bow.
To their own roots.
Fear comes only.
At our invitation but.
It comes. It came.

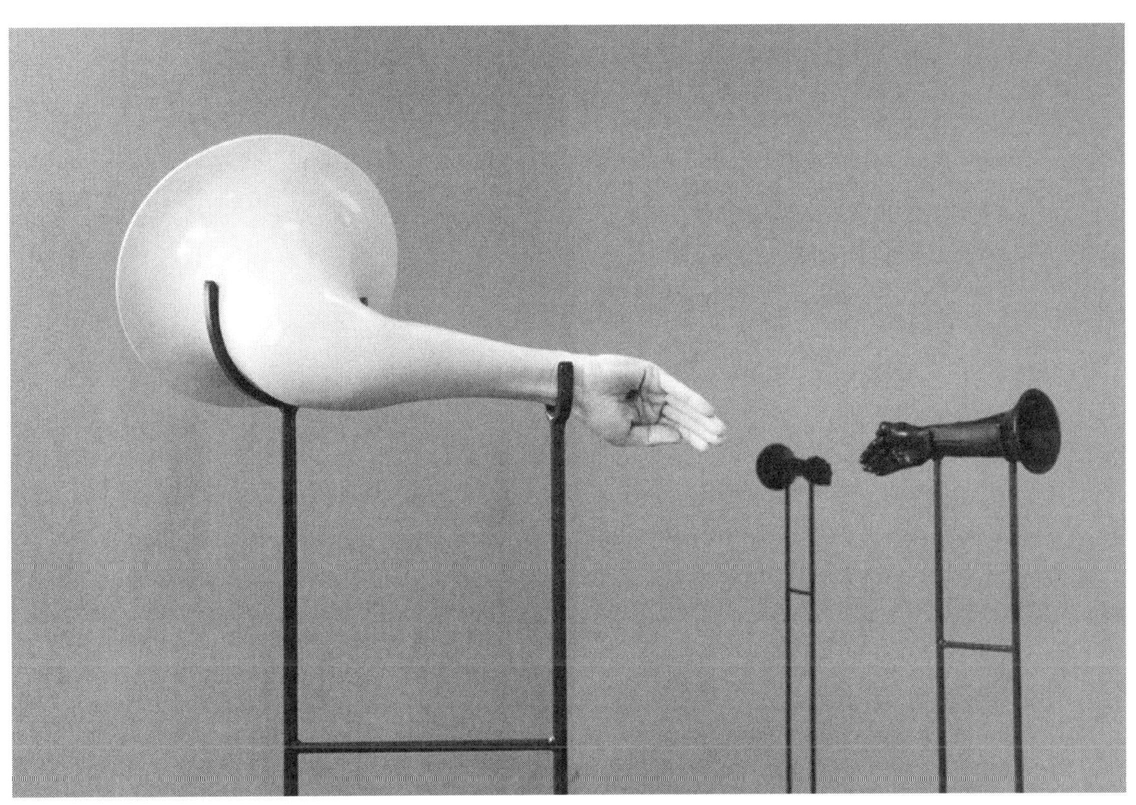

ELANA MANN, *THE ASSONANT ARMORY* (INSTALLATION VIEW), 2016, DETAIL OF THE HANDS-UP-DON'T-SHOOT-HORN AND HISTOPHONE / COURTESY THE ARTIST AND COMMONWEALTH AND COUNCIL, PHOTO: RUBEN DIAZ.

A DISASTER YOU WALK AWAY FROM IS A CALLED A STORY

KAVEH AKBAR

I know what most words mean
and you'll recall I am generally
good with my mouth   you've seen me
use it to drive away myriad
blessings you've watched me use it
to suck up the yolk
from an egg
everything has a touchable
opposite a pile of saltmeat on one side
of a plate and a heap of hair
on the other
          you wouldn't
survive a day in my brain and I wouldn't survive
a second outside it   the tin soldiers
on my windowsill are firing their muskets
into the fog and I can't help but praise
their bravery   as a rule I avoid
windows completely   you can't trust every
person in a neighborhood you can't
even trust their gardens
    there is no
such thing as trapless living
safety's a cudgel we use
to smash away fear

I'm obsessed
with drinking enough water and with
the Vedic hymns when you visit me
I'll teach them to you   their power
is potent if you chant
them enough they can replace
your actual voice like
a drawing you give your father before he leaves
for good
the body is full of entrances
and every person has their favorite I am
most permeable through my eyes I'll believe
anything I see light up
in front of me
here is a drawer
of dry sabzi mailed from Isfahan here is an entire
forest   we can replant what-
ever we burn
there is a veil between us
and the other veils who brought it and
how do we punish them   I am so full
of these questions I apologize in
advance for the way I will
use them to hurt you

ALI LEROI, *I GOT YOU*, 2017

NO ONE GOES TO AMERICA FOR THE FIRST TIME

ANJUM HASAN

I AM IN AMERICA for the first time, and on my first day there I step through a lobby to face a two-storied apartment building running around a swimming pool. The pool is such an unwrinkled blue it looks like a prop, there are empty deck chairs, and in one corner is a barbecue that, too, appears very real and yet unconvincing. *I have seen this before.* In other words, Hollywood.

The setting is from some film I've mostly forgotten. If I search deeper in my memory for more about the film that this scene is evoking — the clean, sunlit pastel of the building, the pool in which no one swims but where someone might be hiding, the unfulfilled promise of the barbecue — then that narrative will take over entirely and any other possible associations — perhaps from a book or painting — are blanked out. But I'm already starting to remember more about the movie featuring these things — that it involves the connected stories of three women, that one of these women will open a door on the upper floor at any moment, lean over the balcony, and jump into the pool, and that this ordinary scene is, therefore, touched with a deep sense of unease. Yet I don't want to give in to it altogether. I don't want déjà vu to harden into recognition.

I go out into the street. A convertible passes slowly down the avenue and the evening sun starts to pink the mildly dusty air between the palm trees in this Los Angeles district of Venice. I have seen this before. The car is driven by a boy visiting from England who doesn't know how to drive. He will careen down the street, the cops will arrive, the scene framed by exactly this broad avenue and this palm-fringed sunset. Later that evening, I am cooking dinner and look out of the kitchen window at the half-lit alley outside to see three large squirelly animals walk across it, not hurried but still furtive and conspiratorial. Raccoons, I think, and they're on their way to steal a man's sports shoes and tear up his carefully laid out lawn. I know how this one ends — with one of the raccoons being deliberately run over. I saw the film in question only a couple of months ago and haven't had a chance to forget the story yet.

And this is how it is over the following days. The afternoon sun slanting through the venetian blinds reminds me of having seen the same brilliantly striped California light framing a man and a woman having a conversation in a room; they are talking about her husband's death, which he, the man with the noirish shadows on his face, will head to Chinatown to investigate. Looking over at a view of Beverly Hills, I'm unable to suppress images of crassly eager teenagers studying video footage of the homes of Hollywood stars so as to plan break-ins while their occupants are out partying. When I am in a bus and the driver confides in me, charmingly, that LA has the most maddening traffic in the world, I am only half listening because in the car before us, stalled in the backed-up early evening jam — the car that the bus driver has just angrily honked at for several seconds — sits a man who has had enough, who is going to step out with his briefcase — a decoy because he's been laid off months ago and isn't really going to work — and have one of Hollywood's most enraged meltdowns.

With time, I find myself trying to dodge the evocations. I would like to see Los Angeles through my own eyes but I find that the city, like that Borgesian book composed entirely of quotations, appears to me wholly derived from films. Some of the films I picture are iconic, of course, but many don't necessarily have the popular mythologies that might encourage visitors to actively map famous scenes onto the city, knowing they were imagined here. *Pulp Fiction*, say. I'm not really seeing *Pulp Fiction* everywhere I go. Instead, many of the films coming to me are old, or obscure, or those a critic might call "forgettable." I have been watching forgettable films for years and now find that I haven't forgotten them at all, that my memory has preserved dozens of minor scenes from even the most trivial films, as if in anticipation of this visit when I might see the real thing. But are the wide boulevards, the bars staffed by aspiring actors, the hills that hide the homes of the rich, the possibility of guns in the glove compartments, the old apartments with art deco motifs the originals? Or the films in which I first saw these things?

The celebrated scholar A. K. Ramanujan said, no Indian reads the Mahabharata and the Ramayana for the first time, which in our era, could well be transmuted into: no Indian goes to America for the first time. An insignificant minority among the middle classes might have resisted going across, a little jaded by the plentitude of America around us, the never-ending appetite for it. But either way, we have already seen the movies and TV shows, read the novels, followed the news headlines, heard out the visiting relatives and friends. So the journey to America is not new for me except in the purely visceral sense of my actually being here. But even this partial newness is received with surprise when I reveal it to the people I meet. No one any longer, it seems, comes to America for the first time. And this only enhances my own bewilderment — the feeling that I am too late, that it is impossible now to experience America as it is. I have to content myself by imagining that the old cliché is true: America is just like the movies.

I am trapped in this persistent déjà vu during my week in LA, which means that I am constantly aware of things being shadowed by another, anterior meaning. But connecting the images before me to the images buried in my memory does not, somehow, resolve this haunted feeling, or vanquish it. The nature of film itself — the way the image on the screen can sear itself onto a receptive mind — has begun to worry me. Could it be the case that I've forgotten *nothing*? Have I become a compendium of everything I've ever seen? A horrifying thought, as much for the character of what one views as for its volume.

I watch movies in a way that can be best described as random: pick them out of one of the plastic crates around the house that my husband keeps loaded, mostly with assorted

Hollywood films, glance at the text on the sleeve and then play it only half knowing what to expect. I watch Hollywood without ever feeling committed to it. I watch it lazily and half-heartedly and yet not without enjoyment, pulled into the story even while noticing how the lifestyle at the edges or in the background of the frame — appliances, clothes, accents, make-up, sexual choices, cars, décor — is the real story. I could be trying to resist Hollywood through Hollywood, imply that I can see these films but I'm not taken in.

Still, I do seem to want this sedation, coming out of this curiously familiar yet remote place, which is why the Hollywood film I am watching doesn't matter so much — it could be forgettable, but for those 90 minutes or so it makes me forget. It is the foreignness that lulls me, the awareness that little of what is unfolding on the screen has anything to do with me, that even if I am fully present in a vicarious sense, I am not obliged to account for what I'm seeing. The corollary to "No one goes to America for the first time" is, of course, we are all Americans now. Yet watching Hollywood, I know full well the separateness of that space called America, a space made up of very distinctive people and buildings and streets and rooms and forests and rivers. The amazing particularity of this world, a particularity reinforced in almost every movie I see, assures me I do not belong to America. I am not *there* and never have been, so I can be a tourist to the country in this way.

This acting out of stories in spaces that are meant to look true-to-life, evoke real locations where real things are happening to real people, is the very opposite of how Bollywood tells its tales. Usually, no city has to look like itself in a Bollywood film, no setting resemble an everyday one. What is the point, these films seem to be asking, if the fantasy of cinema devolved into these all too mundane markers of reality? Everything in such a film tends to contribute not to a realistic effect but an instructive one. All the elements in the frame seem to be shouting out something about the wealth, poverty, beauty, despair, power of the characters. The fashion of putting in Western cities as backdrops and white people as landscape in recent Bollywood blockbusters is only a perversion of a long-standing cinematic convention about the use, or disuse, of place.

So it turns out that the more Hollywood films I watch, the fewer Bollywood films I am able to sit through. I can't fully believe in either but seem to need to suspend much more disbelief for one than for the other. I have ended up falling back on America and becoming aware of just how subliminally its cinema works on me. I discovered with a happy sense of affinity, some years ago, the poet Adil Jussawalla's essay on his painfully intense relationship to films. He was devastated at cartoon tragedies as a child and, as an adult, had to stop watching films altogether because they so completely wrecked him each time. In my own case, I have regulated the drug to one film a week. Any more than that drains me hollow — dialogues rattling with hideous insistence in my head all day and my dreams saturated with scenarios urgently demanding intervention from me. I am embarrassingly out of place in this new era of addictive TV dramas, easy Netflix streaming, and YouTube archives.

Toward the films I do watch, I could take a more intelligent approach: cultivate taste, be more discerning, build a history of viewership. Instead of reaching for just any film, I could follow certain directors or genres, have clearer preferences, seek to impose a bit of my own personality on the overpowering nature of films. I do from time to time attempt this maturity, think of myself as, say, a David Lynch or a David Cronenberg fan, though I sometimes confuse one filmmaker for the other. And what tends to take over very quickly is an awareness of the superfluity of taste. That image on the screen is too much with us. *We have all seen too many films.* This fervidness — this other, insidious way that films work on us — which has nothing to do with what we really like out of what we see, is the thing that becomes clear to me when I go to America for the first time.

Along with *Pulp Fiction*, the film I expected to "see" in Los Angeles was Lynch's well-known *Mullholland Drive*. I kept waiting for it to rear up from the landscape and resonate with my experience of the city. *Mullholland Drive* is, for me, the Hollywood film about Hollywood — about the desire and dread that these films can occasion, and the viewer's complete identification with the fantasy. But my subconscious did not, just because I wanted it to, turn to great cinema. It had other plans. Heading to Hollywood — the geographical location in north Los Angeles, not the indeterminate filmic space in our heads — I completely forgot about David Lynch, instead getting flashbacks to another film — there is a stressed-out movie producer and a trippy painter always dressed in white — about the vanity and mesmerism involved in creating Hollywood.

Strangely, or perhaps predictably, walking down Hollywood Boulevard fills me with a vague excitement but reminds me of nothing. The Hollywood Museum, housed in three narrow floors of an art deco building, is described as the biggest collection of Hollywood memorabilia in the world, which disturbs me. Is this all? I hadn't imagined Hollywood could be domesticated so easily — shuffled into crowded glass cabinets, homey framed autographed portraits, short clips on loop. This is not just too small but too *still* to be a museum of that ceaselessly zooming thing. It hits me hard when I stand before Marilyn Monroe's dress. This is the famous black spangled dress with spaghetti straps that she'd worn on her honeymoon with Joe DiMaggio, a honeymoon she'd interrupted to go and sing voluptuously for the American troops in Korea. This dress was hanging limply on a stand and looking every bit like the worn-out piece of half-century old nylon that it is. There was just nothing to that dress without its cinematically kinetic wearer. (And who moved as much and as fast as Monroe? Forget the dizzying career rise and the repeated firecracker bursts of the marriages. A sign in the museum lists the 40-odd houses she lived in over the less then 40 years of her life.)

In the bus on the way back to Venice, I try to place Monroe in the patchy cache of my movie watching and realize I've only seen one film of hers, a black-and-white one, long ago on late-night television in the early '90s when state-run television in India threw up such things without explanation. It is all set in a hotel room, and I recall Monroe having a painful miscarriage on a bathroom commode while keeping up a conversation with Albert Einstein. When I try to look up the film, I find there is no such thing. Yet I am sure I haven't misremembered — it was Monroe in that trademark off-white halter neck dress and matching slingbacks. More determined, somewhat panicky Googling unearths the answer. The film is actually from 1985, features an actress playing Monroe, and is based on a play that imagines an encounter between her, Einstein, Joseph McCarthy, and Joe DiMaggio. And it is, of course, in color; I had remembered it as black and white only because I'd seen it on our black-and-white set.

When I saw Monroe in all those photographs and clips in that museum, I recognized her but I didn't really know her. Which is exactly what I could say about Hollywood and America at large. My déjà vu shades into recognition even though this isn't the expert's or even the aficionado's knowingness. I am still subject to the whimsies of the images in my head.

That unidentified swimming pool in the courtyard of the apartment where I'm staying continues to bother me. Where have I seen it before? I suddenly remember that I'd exchanged emails about the movie with Jai, a film critic friend. A search through the digital archives of the years turns up the answer: Robert Altman's *3 Women*. The powerful pull of that swimming pool becomes clear to me when I read on Jai's blog, "Generally speaking, water plays a big part in this film, as does the idea of being unnoticed or cocooned. At times you might even be lulled into thinking the whole movie is taking place underwater, or in a place where the usual laws of time and space don't apply. Even when the plot seems to be moving along 'normally', something feels a bit off."

I recall everything now. And yet "something feels a bit off." Perhaps it's another film that I've been trying to get at all along, set in an apartment building exactly like this one, except that now it is night and the place is a motel. A man is in hiding or without a home, and staying in a room on the upper floor. Another man, a friend or lawyer or insurance agent, will come to visit him in that darkness; they have a significant conversation through the screen door and the visitor has this man in his power. I am obsessing now, certain I have seen this film but unable to place it. I've been there, but when? What role did I play? I tell myself, then, that it's just part of one long waking dream, whose images persistently elude even as they seem so compellingly, so discomfitingly, intimate.

THE WAY OF THE DODO

JANET SARBANES

People are always saying, "Well, that went the way of the dodo." Or, as a warning, "Don't go the way of the dodo!" What is the way of the dodo? I will tell you, as I am a dodo.

Until the 17th century, we lived on the island of Mauritius, near Madagascar. We have a history with Dutch sailors — the Dutch were the ones to colonize the island, the sailors were hungry, our rumps were large and inviting. We knew no predators, we were not shy, we had no wings, we couldn't fly. Some think we were hunted to extinction; others, that our eggs — our single eggs, we laid only one, in a nest on the ground — were eaten by the animals the sailors introduced to the island: dogs, pigs, cats, rats. Still others claim to see dodos to this day, deep in the jungles of Mauritius, though they're usually mistaken.

The way of the dodo, then, was simply to be unfit for the New World: too plump, too slow, too trusting. But of this I'm rather proud. Accounts say that when a sailor grabbed ahold of one dodo's leg and it cried out, all of the surrounding dodos came running to its rescue, and so were easily caught. Better to die that way, I say, than live like our cousins the pigeons, who fend for themselves — albeit in great numbers.

KENYATTA A.C HINKLE, *THE EVANESCED #144*, 2016, INDIA INK ON RECYCLED ACID FREE PAPER, 9 X 12 INCHES / COURTESY OF THE ARTIST

HELIOPOLIS AND HELIPAD

JOSHUA CLOVER

I think often of Daslu, the department store in São Paulo that has, I am told, no doors. One enters from the garage below or one helicopters onto the roof. It's like a fucking Bond pic. When I first learned of this it seemed like a missed opportunity for Fredric Jameson, who hinges his epochal *Postmodernism, or, the Cultural Logic of Late Capitalism* on the Bonaventure Hotel in Los Angeles and particularly on its unnavigability, a feature that begins with the challenge of entering the hotel from the street. *You want unnavigability? You want recalcitrance to foot traffic? You should really check out Daslu.*

But that's not quite right. The store corresponds to Jameson's account in some ways. It stands apart from the city that surrounds it, a characteristic Jameson identifies in differing ways with both modernism and postmodernism. Its interior is extravagantly elaborated. And yet, built in the carapace of an old mansion, it does not quite typify the "postmodern hyperspace" that Jameson took as allegory for "the great global multinational and decentered communicational network in which we find ourselves caught as individual subjects." One should not force analogies for the simple reason that any clever person can do it. So I stopped worrying about postmodernism and Jameson's missed opportunity.

But I didn't stop worrying about Daslu. An ominous mansion with no doors is the stuff of nightmare, and it stayed with me. There are other ways to read its design beyond or before sophisticated cultural allegories. Though the heliport is blunt in its testimony, the subterranean garage is even more suggestive, each vehicle inspected by private security for weapons, explosives. What does it mean to fashion an exclusion zone of such rigor that it seems to contravene the very idea of shopping, the compulsions of exchange? Perhaps it is the simple production of exclusivity. And in some sense it is a version of every other poor law, a version of the prohibition on overnight street parking in leafy neighborhoods in the United States designed to make them as hospitable as possible for homeowners and inhospitable for others. But Daslu has an intensity one might almost admire, that seems to make the dialectical leap from quantity to quality of exclusion. It is illiberality armed. The pretense of democracy that provides an ethos for the market — are we not all equal in the moment of exchange? — has no place here.

There are perhaps three million living in São Paulo's *favelas* and *corticos*. The wealth here is global luxury wealth. The poverty is local. Heliópolis, São Paulo's largest *favela* with over 100,000 souls, has 300 books in its library. Like many other slums, it is pushed up directly against high-rise glamour sequestered by gates, walls, security guards. These last most of all. The well-heeled of São Paulo make pervasive use of private security against threat of violence, theft, and kidnapping; they are hustled from house to car by action teams like politicians in a world of potential assassins, played by the *corticados* and *favelados*, the classes dangereuses. And that's all there is. There is no intermediate layer to provide a buffer, to provide persons who might be strolling about town on a Saturday afternoon with a paycheck. There is no middle class for sociologists to obsess over, to put into quintiles, the striated and subtle subclasses that fascinate them. The Foot Traffic For A Luxury Department Store Class is absent; any doors meant for them would be purely vestigial. Maybe you have a chopper at your disposal, maybe you are in a heavy black car, maybe it's armored — or you are hungry. This is the social world mapped by Daslu's design. This is its nonallegorical meaning. Wealth polarization developed to the point where daily life takes on the contours of asymmetrical warfare.

It is easy enough, presented with the theme of revolution, to bemoan its disappearance as a horizon, to despair at the willingness of so-called radicals to throw their arms around the knees of the latest SYRIZA. It is similarly easy to understand how once-revolutionary factions came to be prone in the first place. If there was a systematic global project of the postwar era, it was not "neoliberalism"; it was the annihilation of revolution as a plausible human goal, and the concomitant destruction of any content for the idea of emancipation, until people at the end of human history would associate it with full employment.

But the Pascalian wager of revolution seems no less self-evident: there will be a revolution, a series of them, or the world will end for humans. It has already ended for those condemned to misery, utterly indentured or utterly dispossessed as a condition of birth.

So let us assume there will be a revolution, an emancipatory one, not the kind mentioned often enough by Elon Musk or the Marinho brothers of Grupo Globo. Where might it begin? This is not an easy question, and not one to which we need know the answer in advance. If I had to guess, I would look at places where social antagonism is pitched so high as a practical fact, as a consequence of extreme polarization, that it is already beginning to exceed state management, where the rich are rich enough to hire shooters, and to need them. This is just a guess, one way among many to think about this, but it's a start. Once it pops off, a series of problems will present themselves, not the least of which is how the revolution will sustain itself, cut off from market goods. Brazil, with its prodigious agricultural productivity, offers real possibilities — even if, once the semi-temperate southlands are seized, capitalist organization of production is broken immediately, as one hopes. These are factors we might look for, then: dramatic and increasing use of private security, and ready arable land that can serve as what a friend calls the "belly of the revolution" against the closure of the world market. These are only two coordinates. It unfolds according to many. Neither you nor I will tell it how to unfold. Once begun it will have to spread, of course. Or not spread, exactly, but erupt elsewhere. People will start the day organizing their lives around the free sharing of communal goods, and end the day defending this. Whether people will seize Daslu for a well-fortified outpost or loot it and light it, its fate is sealed.

LOT'S WIFE

SARAH BLAKE

Sure I was a pillar of salt for a minute
but then I was a woman again,

hand still holding the hand of an angel —
I was happy right where I was.

I kissed the angel and the angel
kissed me back like I was the tequila,

the lime, and the salt, all at once.
I could feel the heat of a burning city

to one side of me, the angel's body
to the other, and the winds of the plains

kept pushing that heat into me
like they knew I still had some cold

spots, places that hadn't been touched.
The angel swept me up and hid me

in a cave until we knew everyone
remembered me as Lot's wife, or salt.

Then we built a house we never left.
Everyone thought I was a warning

against sin instead of a woman who
got everything she ever wanted — never

could've known she wanted — until
that angel came down to save me and

licked me like a horse.

LOT'S WIFE'S DREAMING

SARAH BLAKE

Sometimes I'm salt again
Sometimes the wind feels like a man
I didn't say yes to

The world breaks down into minerals
The blood volume of every blooded body
Controlled by the minerals

The question to the men at sea
Always the minerals

And the sea is just a future desert
And the body's just a future desert

The mermaid is taking sea water
In and out her mouth so she's already
Full of salt and made of salt

Sometimes I'm in the sea
Sometimes I am the sea
And I smash a ship and drown the men

Other times I'm sprinkled on a dish
Or added to the butter, with such restraint

ALI LEROI, *THE GREATEST LOVE OF ALL*, 2017

DINAH'S DREAMING

SARAH BLAKE

Any woman's dreamt of killing men.
I dream of strangling one from behind

with a long, soft cloth wrapped tight
around my knuckles, so we're connected —

my joints to his neck, the most tactile
pieces of my body to his breath, his

voice, his Adam's apple, his first seven
vertebrae, his thyroid cartilage, his ache

after too much time spent looking in any
one direction, and his hyoid bone,

which supports the tongue, the tongue
which forms the words, and he says,

Only give me the young woman as my wife.
My fingers hold those words now

to shove into any mouth I like,
and my palms, not cut by any wire,

my hands kept how men like, still able
to sit down to breakfast with my father

and brothers, nothing giving me away,
no blood on the bread.

IN THIS TUESDAY APRIL 4, 2017 FILE PHOTO, ABDEL HAMEED ALYOUSEF, 29, HOLDS HIS TWIN BABIES WHO WERE KILLED DURING A SUSPECTED CHEMICAL WEAPONS ATTACK, IN KHAN SHEIKHOUN IN THE NORTHERN PROVINCE OF IDLIB, SYRIA. TURKEY'S HEALTH MINISTER, RECEP AKDAG SAID TUESDAY, APRIL 11, 2017, THAT TEST RESULTS CONDUCTED ON VICTIMS OF THE CHEMICAL ATTACK IN KHAN SHEIKHOUN CONFIRM THAT SARIN GAS WAS USED. OFFICIALS FROM THE WORLD HEALTH ORGANIZATION AND THE ORGANIZATION FOR THE PROHIBITION OF CHEMICAL WEAPONS PARTICIPATED IN THE AUTOPSIES. (ALAA ALYOUSEF VIA AP, FILE)

TO LOOK OR NOT TO LOOK: IS THAT THE QUESTION?

SARAH SENTILLES

What difference does this photograph make? And what does it mean to look at it?

The man in the photograph — Abdel Hameed Alyousef — sits in the front passenger seat of a car and holds Aya and Ahmed, his nine-month-old twins, dead, wrapped in white cloth, their faces visible. He is on his way to bury them in a mass grave alongside 22 other members of his family, including his wife and brothers, all of whom are reported to have been killed by chemical weapons during an attack in Idlib Province in Syria. Alyousef is not alone. With him are the driver in the front and two men and two young children in the backseat, three of their faces bathed in sunlight. The photographer is there, too, standing outside the car and looking in.

Photographs allow viewers to be somewhere they could not otherwise be, to see what would otherwise remain invisible. The theorist Ariella Azoulay calls photographs "transit visas," and in *The Civil Contract of Photography* she insists the camera grants a kind of citizenship that transcends borders. We are citizens not of nations but of images, she argues. We are accountable to one another, responsible for what we can now see.

But what does this responsibility look like in practice?

Photographs of violence are taken after the violence has occurred, and as a viewer, I have arrived too late. Alyousef's children and most of his family are already dead. Alyousef has already buried them all. This photograph is just one of many photographs of dead and injured children in Syria. Three-year-old Aylan Kurdi washed up on the beach. Five-year-old Omran Daqneesh covered in dust and blood sitting in an ambulance. Yet the violence continues. Borders remain closed to refugees.

In early April 2017, this image rocketed around the internet, appearing on the front page of newspapers, multiplied on Facebook and Twitter feeds. President Trump seemed to refer to this photograph when he said to reporters in the White House Rose Garden, "I will tell you that attack on children yesterday had a big impact on me — big impact. That was a horrible, horrible thing. And I've been watching it and seeing it, and it doesn't get any worse than that." The next evening, speaking from his Florida estate, he said, "Even beautiful babies were cruelly murdered in this very barbaric attack. No child of God should ever suffer such horror."

Then he launched 59 Tomahawk cruise missiles against Syria. Did the photographs do this?

Discussing the video footage of some of those missiles, watching their brightness light up the night, Brian Williams said on MSNBC, "I am tempted to quote the great Leonard Cohen, 'I am guided by the beauty of our weapons.' They are beautiful pictures." Is the photograph of Alyousef a beautiful picture? The bright white cloth in which his dead children are wrapped stands out against his red shirt. The car door cuts through the frame of the photograph, redacting part of the driver's head. The sunlit faces in the backseat are overexposed. The photograph seems to have been taken in haste, a snapshot rather than a composed portrait, closely cropped, urgent.

At what should we look, and from what should we look away? For nearly a decade, I critiqued the aestheticization of suffering. I understood visually pleasing photographs of pain to be ethically suspect. But then I read Susie Linfield's *The Cruel Radiance* and was confronted by the narcissism of my thinking — how it shifts attention away from the content of the photograph and toward the viewer and her emotions, how it reveals a longing to find an innocent space from which to look, or a justification for choosing not to. The debate about whether a photograph of violence should be beautiful "is more concerned with the clear conscience of the viewer than with the plight of the injured subject," Linfield writes. There is no unproblematic way "to show the degradation of a person," she continues. No inoffensive way "to document unforgivable violence." But that's not an excuse not to look.

Which raises the question: What obligation do viewers have when confronted by an image like this?

Photographs bring suffering close, but they can also make it feel further away. Photography can generate otherness. "The more remote or exotic the place, the more likely we are to have full frontal views of the dead and dying," Susan Sontag writes in *Regarding the Pain of Others*, and she's right to point out the racism at the center of such images. The dead who appear in photographs published by the American media are usually from other countries, and in the rare cases when the dead bodies belong to Americans, they are often people of color. Privacy in death — and maybe even dignity — seems reserved for White Americans.

Whose deaths are shown and whose are hidden? When does visibility contribute to accountability for violence, and when does it perpetuate oppression? In "The Condition of Black Life is One of Mourning," Claudia Rankine writes about the devastating decisions made around visibility. Mothers have to decide whether or not to make the bodies of their dead sons visible. The police left Michael Brown's bullet-riddled body in the street for hours, even though his mother cried out for him to be covered. Later, a photograph of Brown's body was published on the front page of *The New York Times*. The police wouldn't let Lesley McSpadden see her son's body, claiming it was evidence, yet, even a casual reader of the news was allowed to look at him.

Emmett Till's mother, Mamie Till Mobley, famously insisted on an open casket to protest the racist violence done to her son. "Let people see what I see," she said. Hers was a decision that turned the lynching tradition against itself, Rankine argues. While photographs of lynched Black bodies circulated as symbols of white supremacy, Mobley displayed her son's body to encourage national grief. "I believe that the whole United States is mourning with me," she said. Who gets to decide who gets to look at whose bodies? Questions about representing Till's murdered body were in the news again after Dana Schutz's controversial painting *Open Casket* was put on display at the Whitney Biennial. You can also visit Till's original coffin at the Smithsonian's National Museum of African American History and Culture, where it rests in a small, shrine-like room, the only place in the museum where taking photographs is not allowed.

Looking at the photograph of Alyousef and his twins, I have to keep reminding myself that the children are dead and not sleeping. Like many viewers, I am perhaps used to images of mothers mourning their children; the Pietà, Mary holding the dead body of Jesus, is one of the most iconic and pervasive images in the history of art. It has been transformed from an image of a particular mother and child into a symbol for human suffering, which risks turning other images of individual mothers and their children into general symbols, too. But this is a photograph of a grieving father, and instead of one adult child, there are two small infants in his arms and two little boys watching from the backseat of a car.

I don't want to look at this image. I wish I hadn't seen it. I'm not sure looking does any good. I want to turn away. But like questions about the aestheticization of suffering, a refusal to view documentary photographs of violence shifts attention away from the pictured atrocity and toward the emotionally affected viewers, as if our sensitivity indicates something about our empathy, as if our turning away signals our essential goodness. The refusal to look also suggests there is a failure at the heart of what Susie Linfield calls "photographic suffering": images are not powerful enough — or, perhaps, they are too powerful, too overwhelming — to effect change. So it's better to close our eyes, better to protect the person in the photograph from our gaze.

But turning away isn't respect, it's denial. We know images effect all kinds of change. Trump looked at this photograph — and presumably at other photographs reported to be even worse — and launched an attack. There's no doubt that images have power. Pornography and advertisements depend on images to make viewers act. If a photograph of suffering doesn't give rise to a sufficient response, perhaps it's not a failure of the picture, but a failure of the viewer. What matters is not *whether* you look. What matters is *how* you look, what kind of witness you become, what you do in response to what you see.

Reports indicate Alyousef wanted this picture to be seen. He positioned his children so they could be captured by the camera. He did not cover their faces. Like Emmett Till's mother, he must have known that after seeing the image viewers will not be able to claim ignorance as an alibi. The challenge, then, is to stay open-eyed, awake. To allow myself to be undone. To refuse to let the camera dehumanize. To see, in Judith Butler's terms, how I am implicated in lives that are not my own. To admit, as Sontag insists, that my privilege is located on the same map as their suffering. To get better at turning intense emotional reactions into political action that stops violence. It doesn't matter what I feel when I look at this photograph. It matters what I do. It matters what I demand my leaders do.

Grief is political, Butler argues in *Precarious Life*. She exposes the hierarchy of grief, the fact that some lives count more than others, that only some deaths are mourned. Recognizing all lives as grievable makes war less possible; it's harder to kill people for whom you will mourn. Photographs can limit grievability, but they can also, like this photograph of Alyousef holding his children, extend it. This photograph is the newest addition to the violent archive, and it won't be the last. Photographs reveal the range of what human beings are capable of doing to and for one another. We kill each other. Yet, like Alyousef holding his children, we also mourn our dead.

THE TOWER

JANET SARBANES

The Tower had always been there, or so the girl believed, since it had been there as long as she could remember, embalmed in a gold metallic substance that once must have dazzled but now gave off a tawdry glow. Though it stood many stories high and filled an entire city block, no one paid it much attention. Except for a slight quickening of pace as they passed the entrance — the Tower doormen were notoriously unpleasant —her mother and father and aunts and uncles simply ignored it. They were serious people, who had lived through wars and exile.

It was fall when she first noticed the Tower growing in height and luster, and that people had begun clustering on the street corners nearby. Some seemed excited — giddy almost — at the Tower's resurgence. Others were troubled —frightened almost. Try as she might, the girl could never get close enough to hear what they were saying; her people stuck to the curb. But each day, the Tower grew taller and brighter, and the babble in the streets grew louder.

That winter, her people avoided the Tower entirely. They couldn't risk falling on the icy patch near the entrance, the way the doormen laughed and jeered at you when you fell — how they sometimes pushed you even — and how the giddy ones piled on, hitting and kicking. Her mother took her the long way home from school, shouldering the wind.

On the first clear day of spring, the girl looked down upon the city and saw a strange sight: little gilded towers had seeded themselves all over, like gold teeth. A tower on every corner, or so it seemed, stretching into a shining rictus many blocks long. Soon after that, a tower went up on her own corner, making the way to and from school even more tortuous. Still her people carried on, serious as ever.

But one day after school, upon making the long trek home with her mother, she found them digging a hole, and climbed down the ladder to help. After that, whenever she ventured out into the city, she came across more excavations. For every tower, there was a hole; for every hole, a tower.

Her family's own hole was warm and dark; they gathered there most evenings. The girl thought this was the way it would be from now on; she didn't know they were tunneling as she slept, tunneling under the towers and finding their way into other holes.

She could've sworn every now and then she saw a tower leaning in the distance, or swaying in the wind, but she didn't believe her eyes until they began to fall. The one on her corner made a sound like tinkling glass when it toppled, but the biggest tower fell with a boom and a great suck of air, into the deep, deep hole that had been prepared for it.

In summer, the dirt was patted down and a park dedicated there, and the serious people smiled to see her skipping over its grave.

AMERIGO VESPUCCI LANDING...

NATALIE SCENTERS-ZAPICO

—1499

A thousand boats I set aflame
on my chest, just to watch them

burn. My knees are caves, my belly
home to a colony

of snakes. If I could walk
this river, the way I walk

through our bedroom, without
clothes, I could conquer

the world. You draw maps
of lands I've never seen

on the palms of my hands.
I push the world together

in prayer, & tear it apart
to wash my hair. All the world's

water is in my eyes. You steal it
by cupping your hands

& raising them to your lips
to drink. When you got

the cartography wrong, you said
we should tear the map

in half, so as not to get confused.
We did. I bled & bled.

KENYATTA A.C HINKLE, *THE EVANESCED #134*, 2016, INDIA INK ON RECYCLED ACID FREE PAPER, 9 X 12 INCHES / COURTESY OF THE ARTIST

MANFRED MÜLLER, *WHITE PRELUDE #382* / © MANFRED MÜLLER, COURTESY OF ROSEGALLERY

MY BROTHER

NATALIE SCENTERS-ZAPICO

climbed a chain-link fence to get to the river. He did not wade into its waters, instead he sat by its brush to witness how dry the river had become. In the sand he found a tin box & inside he found a knife. He hid the knife in his pocket & when he went to climb the chain-link fence to go home, he cut himself in the thigh. He lived for years with an open wound. I'd clean his wound with alcohol & carefully place gauze layer after layer every morning to help him with the pain. When the cut became unbearable I'd sing over his screaming & use manzanilla to calm his eyes red with fever. My brother is still alive & the wound has never healed. It never healed because we willed it so. He hasn't died because we willed it so. The point is not did this really happen to your brother. The point is that this happened to every brother I've ever had. The point is that I've had many brothers. The point is that the land itself hides that which cuts us. The point is that I helped him preserve the infection. I dug my fingers deep in the wound. As long as he screams in pain, I know we're still alive.

TRIANGULO DORADO © DANIEL GONZÁLEZ 2017 @PRINTGONZALEZ

THOU SHALT NOT STEAL BOOKS

DAGOBERTO GILB

I wasn't a book boy. I did have a child's picture book of *Moby Dick*. Probably 25 words a page, very colorful drawings, 30 big pages total? My favorite, and only. I loved it. I have no idea how it got in my possession. I didn't steal it, I say to assure you. Books weren't an item in my home. I remember I did like the glossy-cover encyclopedias they sold, I think it was weekly (could have been monthly), in the supermarkets way back then. I'd persuaded my mom to buy one or two or even three. I never really read them, just liked the idea of them and getting smart if you had them around. I might read a sports page. Mostly scores and stats of especially baseball. I played sports. Whatever was around, whatever anybody wanted to play. I was good at that.

Things changed right after high school. By that I mean for and in me. These were the Vietnam years. Hippies, weed, mushrooms, all as common as long hair (acid seemed to be for nerdy or loony whiteboys who didn't need jobs or come from where they mattered) and those drafted and going, or finally back but a touch wacko and scary. I'd read a book my senior year — by that I mean I tried to — because I was in this special two-hour flunky English class. I thought the teacher was a drunk. Nobody and not me either in this class cared and that's why we were in it. One day this man told those who were listening (or overhearing? I can't remember him talking like a teacher) that hippies read a book called *Stranger in a Strange Land*, that it was like the hippie bible. I don't know where I got it but I don't believe I stole it. I wanted to learn about hippies because I liked marijuana and music and... all that seemed pretty nice about their cute girls and easy life. I didn't get the book at all, what it was about, and I never heard the word "grok" with any of the peoples I encountered then or ever. But I did like that I'd read a book (even if I don't think I did it, really, at least most of it). It made me feel smarter and that seemed...well, good. In the land I'd come up in, it was stupid sucks (the worst of them big and pissed off for being ugly) into scamming or gaming something, and mostly drunk or getting there. I wanted smart.

And so it was either Vietnam or, to stall, junior college. I didn't grow up with my father, a WWII Marine sergeant, but even he, like many, wasn't sure it was a wise move to be a draftee and go there. I kept my full-time employment and went to community college. It was like discovering girls for me. And my world flipped. There wasn't a class I came in knowing anything. I was starving for it all. And I wanted to read the books for class cover to cover. Slow at first, word after word looked up, graph to page to chapter to one after another. There followed books that weren't assigned. Then books others told me about. Then ones I found out about. Books that led to more books.

By the time I transferred to UC Santa Barbara, I thought I was a full-fledged intellectual. I wanted a revolution. I wanted a few. And I stole books. That had nothing to do with a revolution, since I used to steal shit when I didn't know that word and it was candy or beer or gin or albums — those were the gentle things. But it did help to justify it that I was, uh, stealing for the revolution and not me me me. They weren't often even anything to do with revolution. Of course I read Marx, Hegel, Marcuse and Fanon, the Soledad Brothers, Wright, Cleaver. I would steal Camus, Rulfo, Hesse, Paz, Beckett, and Dostoyevsky. Once even Porter (I saw all the pretty English majors carrying around her bestselling collection). Mostly it became stranger books. Because real fast I started changing too. I found I liked all kinds of subjects and titles. Plato to Chuang Tzu to Garcia Marquez and so on. And I wanted everything I read. What is that? That want to own *that* book you read, like it's *yours*?

My favorite bookstore was the Isla Vista Bookstore. I preferred used books, and it had the best quality ones. I spent hours there learning its sections, trying ones in Spanish, trying ones in French. I got into mass westerns, my keeper favorites those when the lead character was an Indian and particularly a half-breed, my specialty. I was such a regular I'd often go there and find a new subject or book and read right there. Sometimes I didn't steal, though mostly that could be seen as strategy — buy one or two real cheap, pants an expensive one or two. And so it was that there was this one pleasant day I'd come in and was wandering around, checking spines and then back covers and a few interior pages. I don't remember where I was, what section, which books. It must have been in a more open area than I usually was. The bookstore had an upper floor that surrounded the main floor, like a gigantic, railed, overhead shelf, where we patrons never went. And maybe I'd been getting so comfortable in there, so used to doing what I did, that I forgot where I was and what I was doing wasn't good: two books down my pants and I looked up (was something said, or all non-verbal alarms?) and the owner was glaring at me. I felt like we knew each other, we approved of each other. I loved his bookstore. So much of my intimate time there. He couldn't help liking me too — he was a bookstore owner, I was the epitome of who and what they were for. Except the stealing part.

I always thought he was Japanese. I don't mean that to imply he was Zen, something as silly as that. Only a California type that did things well and thoughtfully and wasn't messed up as...people like me. He didn't start screaming or calling me names or yelling about police or arrest, didn't rush down to shake or lecture me and cause me to run like a fool. He just stared at me calmly and spoke in a normal voice. "Never come back here again," he said sternly.

I put the stolen books back on their shelf. I creeped off, eyes down, a sicko. I was truly ashamed. And devastated by the loss. I wasn't sure what to do next, where to hide (I couldn't even walk that block for years, pass by), where to be me. I was 50% books, both mind and body.

How many hours or days later I don't remember, but I was in downtown Santa Barbara. I didn't go there so often, just easy to drive to the "city" (I came up in the city of LA) and there was a Mexican restaurant with chilaquiles which always cheered me up. After, I was walking. Not a big town, Santa Barbara was a romantically beautiful one. And I got to what is probably its prettiest public space (as in a 1000 years later antiquity, its monumental center), the courthouse, museum, library. You know how it is when you're walking in the remnants of ancient cities. You sense time and history, your own life in a larger perspective.

I'd never been a book boy young. Back then libraries to me were field trips, where teachers took you every so often and I had to go and, there, be told to shut up. I walked into Santa Barbara's library. There were kind people at desks offering to help me out. Like nurses, or Franciscans blessing this animal, who was me. These library places were still and calm because there was reading going on. People reading, learning, from books. Obvious, right? I know, that simple unless you'd never paid close attention with your brain. For me it was as if I walked into a cathedral, and a sweet hum of wind light was in my ears and turned my eyes both upward and inward.

Okay, that last part didn't happen thus or at all or with sound effects or a light show. Nothing mystical. But I was cured. I mean, I didn't like that I stole books. I stopped. Never again. Like that part of my stupid life was done. Coincided, a little, with me needing to use libraries with stranger books than any bookstore would or could have. My love of books and bookstores and especially IV Bookstore (I'm still ashamed, my penance this) blew up —expanded — to libraries great and small. I've read in a lot of them now, too. Not just UCSB's or UCLA's, not just Santa Barbara's, but ones in El Paso, Austin, Albuquerque, New York, Stanford, the Library of Congress, all these hexagons (what Borges called them) an entrance to an embracing homeland, where I am both innocent and mature over and over, where, good day or bad, sure or confused, I can always imagine I am going to heaven.

JEMIMA WYMAN, *AGGREGATE ICON: PROTESTER PARTICIPATING IN "THE CRUDE AWAKENING" BLOCKADE OF CORYTON OIL REFINERY, STANFORD-LE-HOPE, ESSEX, ENGLAND, 15TH OCTOBER 2010 (STRIPPED MIME)*, 2016, HAND-CUT DIGITAL PHOTOGRAPHS, 20.5 X 20.5 INCHES (FRAMED)

THE MEN WILL CRY

DAVID GORDON

I was meeting Chase at 5 so he could pop my cherry before Daphne's party. But then he texted that his dipshit big brother was home and that was definitely not going to work — us doing it in C's room while that creepy Aspergerish lardass sat gaming and watching porn next door, scratching his wooly butt and sniffing his fingers when he thought no one was looking, stroking his fat little horns. They live in a loft and the walls don't even reach the ceiling. I pictured lying under Chase and opening my eyes to see that round moon face shining down at me. Pitted like the moon with the lumps and scars of acne, glowing like the moon with grease. So Chase found a hotel room online and put it on his Dad's card. He said his Dad's manager just paid the card without question. And since his Dad didn't know Chase had the number, if anyone did notice, he'd just figure he got hacked again. Which he was actually, by Chase, who sold his whole family's identities to this Albanian kid who worked at the shit dollar pizza place and now, every few months, someone tried to buy a phone in Chicago or open up a JCPenney account in Florida. That was the part that cracked Chase up: the look of horror on his stepmom's face when the credit bureau people suggested she might shop at JCP. Not that I've ever seen one either.

We stole some weed from his Mom too. I'm not usually a huge partier but I definitely did not want to be sober for this, and we figured we could just drink for free from the overpriced mini-bar. And snack if we wanted. I had this idea that sex would make you hungry. Like the treadmill since it's aerobic.

We walked across town to the hotel, nymph and faun holding hands. His young horns were still just nubs, soft skin over bone, they hid in his curls and he'd squeak if you squeezed them. I had never shaved. My Mom's hair was fine and blonde, even down there, but my dad is dark. Already the other nymphs at school were either saying I was lucky or bragging about how they shaved and waxed — the waifish dryads, downtown hippy-chic chicks, the curvy, big-boobed naiads who hung by the river and frolicked in bikinis on Snapchat. I was still just a B minus like my Mom so I didn't hold out much hope.

We trod a golden road. It was a winter sunset, swift and soft, like a velvet curtain dropping over the day. But in New York, winter skies can be bright and clear, and now, walking west, we trod a path of gold that spread itself like melting butter, a red carpet premiere unrolling between the hulking shoulders of the buildings that slid into shadow around us. As if, in the dusk, dimly, we saw the future, these clean new towers crumbling and ancient already, listing like broken ships, leaning together like drunken monoliths, head to head on barstools, or sinking into the rising seas that we know will take this island back soon, when the world of men finally subsides into darkness.

Except of course for the windows and storefronts and steel frames that faced west, where the labyrinth of all streets ended. They caught the dying sun and blazed, gleaming like sharpened knives, like shields dripping with the gore that leaked over the horizon, where the slain day was going down like a bull. The bull knelt slowly, it lay down to sleep in the center of the sky, red pooling on the far side of the river now, bleeding orange onto the current, painting the waves. The bull folded its slender, elegant legs, bowing its great horned head, while the blood flowed from the slashes across its belly and open throat.

They said blood, the girls I knew. They said pain. They said it would take forever. They said it would take five seconds because baby was so tight. They said you can't get pregnant the first time. They said they knew a girl who did. You will feel like a real woman. You will lie down a child and get up one step closer to no longer being a girl, without innocence, that sealed flower. And even as a flower blooms it is already losing its freshness. They said you will not cum. They said you will cry.

But tonight, it is the men who will cry.

The hotel is a big glass box and we get a southwest room. Some airline had it booked and no one used it so they can resell it now to us cheap. Chase gets a beer from the fridge and goes into the bathroom. Wow look at this he says stepping into the glass shower fully dressed with his shoes on, just two walls and a door in the corner, abutting a half-frosted window from which the city lights can be seen blinking on, one by one. Then he shuts the door to pee, I guess, and I think, isn't that odd how we will be like connecting our genitals any moment but we still don't want anyone to see pee coming out of them? Well, some people do but you know what I mean. I hit the mini-bar, downing a little baby vodka bottle. Then I feel sort of ill and chase it with Diet Coke. But then I feel the buzz and I'm okay. I take off all my clothes and stand naked in the full-length mirror that covers one wall. (The other wall is glass and now it is nighttime. The sun is down and the river is black, pale glimmers floating where the light touches, like a hand stroking silver-black fur. No moon is visible from here.) I look okay, I guess. I am not thrilled with my thighs but whatever. I stand in different positions, one leg forward, then the other, hip rotated, weight on the back foot, trying to strike the best pose for when he comes out, but when I hear the toilet flush, I panic and hop under the covers. Nothing happens though, and I wait and wait, drinking another baby vodka, but this time in little nips along with the Diet Coke.

Chase comes out, still dressed.

"What the fuck?" I tell him. "Get naked. Let's get this over with."

He nods and strips. His young skin is nearly as hairless as mine. Except for the thatch of black in his crotch, as if a bird had built a nest in the crook between his legs. The head of his penis bobs like a bald hatchling, working its tiny mouth, crying for mush.

"What are you smiling at?" he asks.

"Nothing. Come on." I peel the blanket back and he slides under. We start making out which is nice and with the booze in me I am getting kind of turned on. But then I reach down and he is still totally soft, like an unblown balloon.

"Why aren't you hard?"

He shrugs. "Give it a second. It's not like an automatic machine."

"I thought it was." I put his hand between my thighs. "Come on," I say while I tug him. "You have to get me wet first too."

"It gets wet?!" Chase looks amazed. "Why?"

"It just does. I guess so that you like slide in easier?"

"Wow. That's cool I guess."

"You didn't know that? Don't you watch porn?" (Spoiler alert: This should have been a clue but whatever.) I ask him, "How do you think Ione and Clio and Asia all sell their panties? Think about it. Would those old dudes pay 50 bucks a pop for dry panties?" The Nerieds got this business started when Clio posted an ad for Moist & Fragrant Schoolgirl Nymph Panties. I never got involved because, one, you had to meet the guy and turn them over — not literally *in* them, though with pervy Asia I wonder — just like meet at Starbucks with them in a bag. But still. Creepy. And two, how would I explain the constant missing underwear to my Mom?

"Duh," Chase says. "They just buy really cheap new ones, wear them and sell them, like a separate special batch. Dumbass."

"Fine," I say. "But at least I know moist panties are wet."

We fool around some more, but nothing doing, so I go down on him and that, I must say, is pretty weird. I've gone down on guys a few times before but I've never held like a soft head in my mouth. I feel like a fish nibbling a worm on a hook.

"What's going on?" I ask him. He doesn't move at all. He lies perfectly still. Now I am feeling kind of weirded out and lie flat on my back, eyes shut. He rolls over, back to me. I am completely embarrassed, I can feel my face burning, so I ask, "I mean, am I totally gross to you or what?"

"No. You're hot I swear," he says. He mumbles it though, curled up in a ball, and I can hear the catch in his throat.

"Holy shit. Are you crying?"

"No," he says but I can tell that he definitely is. I am relieved. Now I know, this is not going to happen and it is not my fault. I rub his back.

"Hey don't worry. I've heard about this happening. You probably drank too much. Or it's the weed."

"It's not that," he says, clearing his throat. It is dark in the room. Day is long gone and we have not turned on the lights.

"Then what?"

"I don't think I like girls after all," he says, with a nervous chuckle. "Sorry. My bad."

"What?" Now I am annoyed. "I thought you were bi-curious?"

"I am. I mean I was, but now my curiosity about girls is satisfied."

"Thanks."

"That's not what I mean." He turns over to face me, and I turn on my side to face him in the gloom. "You know I think you're beautiful. Your new haircut is so amazing. And you have the best butt of any white girl in our grade. How did I know I only like men? I'm a virgin. I mean, maybe I won't like guys either."

"So you're changing your status to gay?"

"Yeah I guess. Sorry."

"Great. Just my luck. I fucking cured you of being straight."

We go online. Chase dares me to post V-card for sale and I get like 1,000 answers in 30 seconds. The knobbly dicks and leering old faces pile up so fast — offers into the low four figures — that I'm afraid of crashing the internet and I shut it down. He goes on Grindr and finds a guy in the bar downstairs. The dude, I admit, is fucking hot, like underwear-model level, a true demigod. Chase invites him up. But he is still nervous and I am kind of drunk with no place to go so I take some pillows and hide in the closet with my phone and my earbuds and listen to a rap mix and peek.

It happens fast. The guy comes in and they talk a while, though I can't hear what they're saying. They make out and feel each other's arms, chests, bulges. Then the demigod stands up and strips, he is like mega-buff with rippling abs and thighs like greyhounds, sleek and twitching to run. His cock is fat and hairless, but uncut, so it looks like a blind headless larva or something to me, but Chase is into it I guess, because right away he is on it, sucking like a thirsty bum on a 40. Bi my ass. Chase gets naked too and the guy goes down on him, and I admit his head game is much tighter than mine. Then demi goes to his jacket and gets out lube and a condom. He fingers Chase awhile and then it's on. I turn down my volume. I am surprised to see he takes him from the front. (Didn't know that was an option for anal!) I can't see much. I can hear Chase howl and I gasp, but luckily the dude can't hear. He says to Chase that it will feel better soon, and I guess it does because Chase stops groaning and starts moaning. Then his head turns on the mattress and I see he's crying. Again! Tears run sideways over his face. Now what? Is it for like joy this time or because his ass is killing him? I mean, girls talk about how losing it will hurt but I have never truly gone there mentally with the butt. The guy doesn't notice because his eyes are shut tight and he is I guess in the zone, with a terrible look on his face, and then he groans super hard and I realize this is first time IRL that I have seen a full-grown man nut. His face is both tragic and comic. Like a mask of agony and rage, straining over my splayed friend like Achilles kneeling over the corpse of his beloved friend, Patroclus, howling, ecstatic in grief, or driving his chariot, crying out in horror and triumph, dragging the body of Hector around the walls of Troy. They say even the river god Scamander tried to drown Achilles because he choked the waters with all the men he slayed.

Then I realize my legs are asleep. I try to gently unfold them, but I spaz out and my foot jerks forward, kicking the closet door open and I am face to face with demi, the grossly loaded condom dangling from his deflating horn. The look on his face is pure terror. "WHAT THE HELL IS THIS?!?! WHO ARE YOU?!?!" His yell is a lot higher and no offense gayer then I thought when I saw his superhard bod and manly scruff. He covers himself, cowering. Chase looks up, sees me, and shouts, "OLLIE WHAT THE FUCK!!!" The guy is like stumbling to put his clothes on, yanking up his boxer-briefs with the rubber still drooping off his thing like a fake nose at Halloween. I want to tell him but now I am laughing uncontrollably and just point. He takes it the wrong way and thinks I am mocking him. "IS THIS A PRANK ARE YOU TAPING THIS?!?!" He is seriously freaking. Now Chase is laughing too, having morphed from crying. Anyway, the guy gets aggro for a minute worried I was like filming him, (as if I want to see that again!) and then runs off, all worried about what if his husband found out. So I don't mention the rubber. Fuck him. Cheater.

Chase takes a shower and comes out in a fluffy white robe. I ask him if his butt is sore and he says yes so I give him the lip balm from my bag and while he like applies it discreetly I ask him, so was that fun because it looked painful?

"It was more than fun Olivia," he says in a mature tone, like he is an adult now. "It was transformative." I want to ask why he cried then but he changes the subject, all worked up about it being my turn, and even though I'm starting to feel sort of over the whole thing, he is insistent, and I figure a deal's a deal. So we speedswipe and there's this dude, like twentysomething, sort of cute. I write back demanding a nude, or Chase does, typing for me. We are in our undies side by side on the bed and I realize how chill that feels now that we have admitted there is absolutely no sexual chemistry between us at all. Like I finally feel relaxed around a guy only if I know he doesn't want me when every day I wonder if they do. I want to know I can make their dicks rise up, like a snake charmer, or psychic powers bending a spoon. But maybe that is all I want for now.

The dude sends the pic back and he is kind of hot. Chase says his dick is a good shape and nicely sized but not too big. It looks big enough to me considering where it's going, but I say okay and he tells the guy to come over. Now Chase will hide in the closet, for safety reasons, though if the guy does turn out to be psycho, I'm not sure what he can do. Call 911 from the closet? It would be faster to just call room service, order a steak dinner for the knife.

When the dude arrives he looks younger than I had imagined, or perhaps simply more nervous and less confident and so, more childlike. His nose for example is tiny, an open plug, twin holes above the round mouth. His lips are moist and red. And I am not eager to kiss them. I see this is going to be rough so I get out two more little bottles, the vodka's gone so rum for me and whiskey for him, and we toast and down them. Then I start taking off my clothes and he does too. Then he tries to kiss me and I let him though my lips are cold and his are, as I feared, warm and wet, his tongue like a fish lashing in my mouth. But at least he is hard. I lie down and he is so fixated on the space between my legs that I am embarrassed, for him not myself, and look away at our doubles in the mirror. I ask if he has a condom and he nods. Gets it out with feverish shaking hands. Rips the foil and rolls it on and I suddenly think: like a surgeon getting ready to operate on a prone body. He climbs aboard. Again he tries to kiss me and I turn my head back to the mirror. This is where it all goes wrong. I should have been watching, I guess. Or lent a hand. Instead, he is already on me, and starting to hump away, when I realize, I don't think he is actually inside. But his weight is pressing on me and he is bouncing up and down too hard to notice when I tap him on the shoulder. The whole bed shakes. He is sweating now and rocking up and down and his wet red fishy mouth is breathing and spraying into my ear, and then I hear him moaning, I love you I love you. Get off me, I say but he can't hear me because he is crushing my lungs and I can barely breathe, much less make sounds. I am basically coughing out the words, exhaling them: Cough me, cough me. Then he sort of collapses on top of me, like a log, and I realize he is weeping because there are tears running down into the pink shell of my ear now, filling it like a little bone teacup, and leaking maybe into the maze of my brain where they will stain my dreams for years. I slap his back, trying to wriggle free as he hugs me tighter, maybe thinking I am trying to cuddle, and kisses my neck with those wet lips. Help, I cough at the mirrored closet door. Help, I gasp at my own face. Finally the dude turns his head and sees Chase standing over us.

"Hey! Hey!" He jerks back terrified. "Who are you?"

Chase brandishes a shoe-tree he apparently found in the closet. "I'm her fucking boyfriend! Who are you?"

The dude gets his clothes on and is out of there quick. "How was it?" Chase asks me after. "Okay," I say and shrug. "Cool," he says. Technically I realize I am probably still a virgin, maybe, but I don't want to get into it, so I leave that out. "Should we go to the party?" he asks. "Okay," I say. "Cool. Let me just rinse off and we'll go."

Thing is I am pretty drunk by now, so we uber to the party, and it is loud and everybody is yelling at each other over the music and a small knot of kids are dancing in silence, not touching, each one staring off into her own head, and Chase announces that we both are de-virginized, kind of letting them all still think it was with each other, and he high-fives and I don't disabuse anyone, about either my cherryness or his gayness, and right away Daph smokes us up in her room as a token of her esteem and next thing I know I am out flat on her pillows and in my dream I ride a white horse through a magic wood where the soul of each tree, each rock, each spring is reaching out to me as I rush by, and I do not know if my horse and I slip through because their hands are the hands of ghosts and cannot touch, or because we are a dream, my horse and I, and cannot be touched, my hair blowing like the white mane streaming ghost-white through the forest, like gray blunt smoke through my fingers, long blond hair weaving and unweaving itself in the teeth of time's comb.

The trees turned slowly, to and fro, as if they had lost their way in the mist and were reaching out as far as they could, but unable to touch each other, too afraid to move. They raise their limbs in silent pleading as we pass. The silvered moonlight lying on their bark shines like glitter makeup running with tears.

I head home later, alone and on foot, but then realize I still have the key card to the room and it is booked till 11 a.m. It is one. I am sober now and except for a slight ache my mind is clear. I'm hungry and room service on Chase's Dad sounds good. So I go back to the hotel and am walking through the lobby when I see a handsome satyr with a wedding ring and black hair on the backs of his hands. His long handsome face is rough with gray and black stubble and there are iron gray veins running through the curly black hair between his horns. He smiles at me with crooked teeth and on impulse I smile back and head into the bar. He follows, as I know he will, and buys me a drink. He is talking, laughing, calm and low, but his hand is on my elbow, just naturally, then on my knee and I let it be there. He asks if I'm staying at the hotel and I hand him my keycard just like that.

We go upstairs. We get undressed and at least he is a better kisser, nipping my lips softer and then harder, like bites with your fangs retracted, and my fingers feel good moving through the tangle of hair on his chest. I ask him to turn off the light and when he does, night appears in the window and I realize it is snowing outside, tiny points of white static, like white moths swarming and swimming behind the glass. Like an aquarium, but I am the one underwater. Or in outer space, I think, lying there on my side and staring out at the black river, toward the invisible shore, while countless stars travel for lightyears just to die against our glass, like bugs against a windshield, headlight-haloed, when we're driving, fast, at night. It is as if we were the last of our kind, I think, nymph and satyr on a starship with the power gone, drifting through the Leonids shower, as he puts his hand on my hip, and I cannot see if he is crying or not as I turn to face him in the dark.

LARB presents a participatory artist project by Meghann McCrory, in collaboration with The Constituents, a Los Angeles-based volunteer group focused on promoting civic engagement and voter education.

To learn more visit: theconstituentsla.com

We invite you to send the postcard included in this issue of LARB to one of your elected representatives.

From the White House to City Hall, make your voice heard.

To find out who your local, state and federal elected representatives are, go to bit.ly/yourrepsLA

Include your zip code on your postcard so your reps know you are a constituent.

FEDERAL:

President Donald Trump
The White House
1600 Pennsylvania Avenue NW
Washington, DC 20500

Vice President Mike Pence
The White House
1600 Pennsylvania Avenue NW
Washington, DC 20500

US SENATE:

Sen. Dianne Feinstein
331 Hart Senate Office Building
Washington, DC 20510

Sen. Kamala Harris
112 Hart Senate Office Building
Washington, DC 20510

US HOUSE OF REPRESENTATIVES:

US Rep. Judy Chu – 27th District
2423 Rayburn House Office Building
Washington, DC 20515

US Rep. Adam Schiff – 28th District
2372 Rayburn House Office Building
Washington, DC 20515

US Rep. Tony Cárdenas – 29th District
1510 Longworth House Office Building
Washington, DC 20515

US Rep. Brad Sherman – 30th District
2181 Rayburn House Office Building
Washington, DC 20515

US Rep. Grace Napolitano – 32nd District
1610 Longworth House Office Building
Washington, DC 20515

US Rep. Ted Lieu – 33rd district
236 Cannon House Office Building
Washington, DC 20515

US Rep. Jimmy Gomez – 34th District
1226 Longworth House Office Building
Washington, DC 20515

US Rep. Norma Torres – 35th District
1713 Longworth House Office Building
Washington, DC 20515

US Rep. Karen Bass – 37th District
2241 Rayburn House Office Building
Washington, DC 20515

US Rep. Ed Royce – 39th District
2310 Rayburn House Office Building
Washington, DC 20515

US Rep. Lucille Roybal-Allard – 40th District
2083 Rayburn House Office Building
Washington, DC 20515

US Rep. Maxine Waters – 43rd District
2221 Rayburn House Office Building
Washington, DC 20515

US Rep. Nanette Barragán – 44th District
1320 Longworth House Office Building
Washington, DC 20515

STATE:

Governor Jerry Brown
c/o State Capitol, Room 1173
Sacramento, CA 95814

Attorney General Xavier Becerra
California Department of Justice
Attn: Public Inquiry Unit
P.O. Box 944255
Sacramento, CA 94244-2550

CA SENATE:

Sen. Bob Hertzberg – 18th District
State Capitol, Room 4038
Sacramento, CA 95814

Sen. Kevin de León – 24th District
State Capitol, Room 205
Sacramento, CA 95814

Sen. Anthony Portantino – 25th District
State Capitol, Room 3086
Sacramento, CA 95814

Sen. Benjamin Allen – 26th District
State Capitol, Room 5072
Sacramento, CA 95814-4900

Sen. Henry I. Stern – 27th District
State Capitol, Room 3070
Sacramento, CA 95814

Sen. Holly Mitchell – 30th District
State Capitol, Room 5080
Sacramento, CA 95814

Sen. Ricardo Lara – 33rd District
State Capitol, Room 5050
Sacramento, CA 95814

Sen. Steven Bradford – 35th District
State Capitol, Room 2062
Sacramento, CA 95814

CA STATE ASSEMBLY:

Assemb. Raul Bocanegra – 39th District
P.O. Box 942849
Sacramento, CA 94249-0039

Assemb. Chris Holden – 41st District
P.O. Box 942849
Sacramento, CA 94249-0041

Assemb. Laura Friedman – 43rd District
P.O. Box 942849
Sacramento, CA 94249-0043

Assemb. Matthew Dababneh – 45th District
P.O. Box 942849
Sacramento, CA 94249-0045

Assemb. Adrin Nazarian – 46th District
P.O. Box 942849
Sacramento, CA 94249-0046

Assemb. Richard Bloom – 50th District
P.O. Box 942849
Sacramento, CA 94249-0050

51st District – Currently Vacant
Special Election to be held in 2017

Assemb. Miguel Santiago – 53rd District
P.O. Box 942849
Sacramento, CA 94249-0053

Assemb. Sebastian Ridley-Thomas – 54th District
P.O. Box 942849
Sacramento, CA 94249-0054

Assemb. Reginald Byron Jones-Sawyer, Sr. – 59th District
P.O. Box 942849
Sacramento, CA 94249-0059

Assemb. Autumn Burke – 62nd District
P.O. Box 942849
Sacramento, CA 94249-0062

Assemb. Mike Gipson – 64th District
P.O. Box 942849
Sacramento, CA 94249-0064

CITY:

Mayor Eric Garcetti
200 N. Spring Street
Los Angeles, CA 90012

CONTRIBUTORS

Sara Ahmed is a feminist writer, scholar, and activist. She is the author of *Willful Subjects* (2014), *On Being Included* (2012), *The Promise of Happiness* (2010), and *Queer Phenomenology* (2011). Her most recent book is *Living a Feminist Life* (2017).

Kaveh Akbar is the founding editor of *Divedapper*. His poems have appeared recently or will soon in *The New Yorker*, *Poetry*, *Ploughshares*, *APR*, *Tin House*, and elsewhere. His debut full-length collection, *Calling a Wolf a Wolf*, will be published by Alice James Books in September 2017; he is also the author of the chapbook *Portrait of the Alcoholic*. The recipient of a Ruth Lilly and Dorothy Sargent Rosenberg Poetry Fellowship from the Poetry Foundation and a Lucille Medwick Memorial Award from the Poetry Society of America, Kaveh was born in Tehran, Iran, and is a Visiting Professor of Poetry in the Purdue University MFA program.

Sarah Blake is the author of *Mr. West* and the forthcoming collection, *Let's Not Live on Earth* (both from Wesleyan University Press). An illustrated workbook accompanies her first chapbook, *Named After Death* (Banango Editions). In 2013, she was awarded a literature fellowship from the NEA. She lives outside of Philadelphia with her husband and son.

Joshua Clover is the author of *Riot.Strike.Riot: The New Era of Uprisings* (Verso 2016) and *Red Epic* (Commune Editions 2015).

J.D. Daniels drove through North Dakota, South Dakota, Nebraska, Kansas, Oklahoma, and Texas before the 2016 US Presidential Election; his report appears in the May 2017 issue of *Esquire*. His collection *The Correspondence* was published by Farrar Strauss and Giroux in January 2017, by Jonathan Cape UK in April 2017, and is forthcoming from Suhrkamp Verlag.

Colin Dayan is Robert Penn Warren Professor in the Humanities and Professor of Law at Vanderbilt University. She is the author most recently of *With Dogs at the Edge of Life*. Her other books include *The Law is a White Dog: How Legal Rituals Make and Unmake Persons; The Story of Cruel and Unusual; and Haiti, History, and the Gods*. She is currently completing a memoir.

Andrew Durbin is the author of several chapbooks, including *Reveler* and *Believers*. His work has appeared in the *BOMB*, *The Boston Review*, *Fence*, *Mousse*, *Triple Canopy*, and elsewhere. He co-edits *Wonder* and lives in New York.

Lina María Ferreira Cabeza-Vanegas graduated with both a creative nonfiction writing and a literary translation MFA from the University of Iowa. She is the author of *Drown Sever Sing* from Anomalous press and *Don't Come Back*, from Mad River Books, an imprint of the Ohio State University Press. Her fiction, nonfiction, poetry and translation work has been featured in journals including *The Bellingham Review*, *The Chicago Review*, *Fourth Genre*, *Brevity*, *Poets & Writers* and the *Sunday Rumpus* among others. She won the Best of the Net, the Iron Horse Review's Discovered Voices Award, has been nominated for multiple Pushcart Prizes and is a Rona Jaffe fellow. She moved from Colombia to China to Columbus to Richmond, Virginia where she works as an assistant professor for the Virginia Commonwealth University.

Dagoberto Gilb is the author of nine books. Among his writing's honors are the PEN/Hemingway Award, a Guggenheim fellowship, and a Whiting Writer's Award. His fiction and nonfiction have appeared a number of times in *The New Yorker*, *Harper's*, and *Best American Essays*. He is also the founding editor of the literary magazine *Huizache*.

Anjum Hasan is the author of the novels *The Cosmopolitans*, *Neti, Neti*, and *Lunatic in my Head*, the short story collection, *Difficult Pleasures*, and the book of poems, *Street on the Hill*. She lives in Bangalore.

Ignacio M. Sánchez Prado is a professor of Spanish and Latin American Studies at Washington University in Saint Louis. His research focuses on the relationship between aesthetics, ideology, and cultural institutions in Mexico, with a particular focus on literature and cinema. He is the author of *El canon y sus formas. La reinvención de Harold Bloom y sus lecturas hispanoamericanas* (2002), *Naciones intelectuales. Las fundaciones de la modernidad literaria mexicana (1917-1959)* (2009), winner of the LASA Mexico 2010 Humanities Book Award: *Intermitencias americanistas. Ensayos académicos y literarios (2004-2009)* (2012), *Screening Neoliiberalism. Transforming Mexican Cinema 1988-2012* (2014), and *Strategic Occidentalism. "World Literature," Mexican Fiction and the Neoliberalization of the Book Market* (forthcoming in 2018).

Hooman Majd is a writer based in New York, and an NBC News contributor. He has written for publications including the *New York Times, The Guardian, The New Yorker, Vanity Fair, The Financial Times, GQ, Time,* and *Newsweek*, among others, and is the author of New York Times bestseller *The Ayatollah Begs to Differ* (Doubleday), *The Ayatollahs' Democracy* (Norton),*and The Ministry of Guidance Invites You to Not Stay* (Doubleday). His short fiction has been published by *Serpents Tail* (UK), as well as in the journals *Bald Ego, The American Scholar, and Guernica.*

Evelyn McDonnell is associate professor of journalism and new media at Loyola Marymount University. She has been writing about popular culture and society for more than 20 years. She is the author of four books: *Queens of Noise: The Real Story of the Runaways*; *Mamarama: A Memoir of Sex, Kids and Rock 'n' Roll*; *Army of She: Icelandic, Iconoclastic, Irrepressible Bjork*; and *Rent* by Jonathan Larson. She is series editor for *Why Music Matters* at ForeEdge Press. She has been the editorial director of www.MOLI.com, pop culture writer at *The Miami Herald*, senior editor at *The Village Voice*, and associate editor at *SF Weekly*. Her writing on music, poetry, theater, and culture has appeared in numerous publications and anthologies, including the *Los Angeles Times, Ms., Rolling Stone, The New York Times,* and *Spin*. She leaves in San Pedro with her husband, son, many animals, and a fantastic view of the ocean.

George Prochnik is a writer and editor. His most recent book, *Stranger in a Strange Land: Searching for Gershom Scholem and Jerusalem* was a *New York Times* "Editor's Choice." His previous book, *The Impossible Exile: Stefan Zweig at the End of the World*, received the National Jewish Book Award for Biography/Memoir in 2014.

Janet Sarbanes is the author of the short story collection *Army of One*, hailed by BOMB as a "stingingly funny fiction debut." Her newest collection is *The Protester Has Been Released* (C & R Press, 2017). Recent short fiction appears in *Black Clock, P- Queue, Entropy* and *North Dakota Quarterly*. Sarbanes has also published art criticism and other critical writing in museum catalogues, anthologies, and journals such as *East of Borneo, Afterall, Journal of Utopian Studies* and *the Los Angeles Review of Books*. She lives in Los Angeles and teaches in the MFA Creative Writing Program at CalArts.

Natalie Scenters-Zapico is the author of *The Verging Cities*, winner of the 2017 PEN/Joyce Osterweil Award, 2016 GLCA Award, 2015 National Association of Chicana/o Studies Book Award, and the 2015 Utah Book Award (Center for Literary Publishing 2015.) Her most recent poems have appeared in *Poetry, Boston Review*, and the Academy of American Poets' *Poem A-Day*. She is Poet-In-Residence at Westminster College.

Rebecca Schiff graduated from Columbia University's MFA program, where she received a Henfield Prize. Her stories have appeared in *n+1, Electric Literature, The American Reader, Guernica, The Guardian*, and *Lenny Letter*. She lives in Brooklyn.

Sarah Sentilles is a writer, critical theorist, scholar of religion, and author of several books, including *Breaking Up with God: A Love Story*. Her most recent book, *Draw Your Weapons*, was published by Random House. She earned a bachelor's degree at Yale and master's and doctoral degrees at Harvard. At the core of her scholarship, writing, and activism is a commitment to investigating the roles language, images, and practices play in oppression, violence, social transformation, and justice movements. She has taught at Pacific Northwest College of Art, Portland State University, California State University Channel Islands, and Willamette University, where she was the Mark and Melody Teppola Presidential Distinguished Visiting Professor.

Danez Smith is a Black, queer, poz writer & performer from St. Paul, Minnesota. Danez is the author of *Don't Call Us Dead* (Graywolf Press, 2017) and *[insert] boy* (YesYes Books, 2014), winner of the Kate Tufts Discovery Award, the Lambda Literary Award for Gay Poetry, and the John C. Zacharis Award from Ploughshares. They are the recipient of fellowships from the Poetry Foundation, the McKnight Foundation, and is a 2017 National Endowment for the Arts Fellow. Danez's work has been featured widely including in on *Buzzfeed, Blavity, PBS NewsHour, Best American Poetry 2017*, and on *The Late Show with Stephen Colbert*.

Jervey Tervalon is an award winning poet, screenwriter and dramatist. His debut novel *Understand This*, won the 1994 New Voices Award from the Quality Paperback Book Club. He has contributed to *The Los Angeles Times, Details* and other publications. He lives in California with his wife and child and teaches creative writing at California State University at Los Angeles.

FEATURED ARTISTS

Danielle Dean was born to a Nigerian father and an English mother in Alabama and brought up in a suburb of London in the U.K. Her work focuses on the processes of construction of race, gender, age and class that are generated through target-marketing practices and commodifying subjectivities. Danielle studied Fine Art at Central St Martins in London and received her MFA from California Institute of the Arts. She has been a Whitney Independent Study Program Fellow in New York City and a participant at the Skowhegan School of Painting and Sculpture in Maine. Solo exhibitions include Hexafluorosilicic and PTL (Part Time Lover) at Commonwealth and Council, Los Angeles; and Confessions on a Dance Floor, The Bindery Projects, Minnesota. Group shows include Made in L.A. 2014, The Hammer Museum; Demolition Woman, Guggenheim Gallery at Chapman University, Orange County; and Auto Italia South East, London.

Daniel Gonzalez is an artist and printmaker living in Highland Park, CA. His formal training as an artist started when he was 12 and enrolled into the Academia de arte Yepes, a free art school held in the basement of Salesian High School in East L.A. At 18, Gonzalez was accepted to the California College of Arts and Crafts, where he studied graphic design for two years. While there, he was introduced to printmaking and the letterpress through volunteer work at the San Francisco Center for the Book and the Mission Cultural Center. His work is inspired by the folk stories that his parents and grandparents have passed on. want to be able to communicate through the image an invitation to tell a new story to be told or an old one to be remembered.

Kenyatta A.C. Hinkle is an interdisciplinary visual artist, writer and performer. Her practice fluctuates between collaborations and participatory projects with alternative gallery spaces within various communities to projects that are intimate and based upon her private experiences in relationship to historical events and contexts. A term that has become a mantra for her practice is the "Historical Present," as she examines the residue of history and how it affects our contemporary world perspective. Her artwork and experimental writing has been exhibited and performed at The Studio Museum in Harlem, Project Row Houses, The Hammer Museum, The Museum of Art at The University of New Hampshire, The Museum of the African Diaspora (MoAD) in San Francisco and The Made in LA 2012 Biennial. Hinkle's work has been reviewed by the *Los Angeles Times, LA Weekly, Artforum, Hyperallergic, The Huffington Post, The Washington Post* and *The New York Times.* She is also the recipient of several awards including: The Cultural Center for Innovation's Investing in Artists Grant, Social Practice in Art (SPart-LA), Jacob K Javits Fellowship for Graduate Study, The Fulbright Student Fellowship, and The Rema Hort Mann Foundation's Emerging Artists Award.

Sanaz Khosravi was born in Tehran, Iran, in 1990. In 2007, at the age of 17, she moved to the United States. She is currently studying Practice of Art (BA) at the University of California, Berkeley. Sanaz's work aims to create imageries of femininity in the contemporary world. Her works confront the social issues while focusing on hope in everyday life. She uses the power of art to touch the hearts and minds of people in order to inspire social changes in her home country and around the world.

Ali LeRoi is a television producer/director and photographer. His recent photographic work is an exploration of his connection to humanity and a record meant to expand the catalog of the black experience. "What Are We Fighting For?" is a group of images that suggest that the first revolution is the revolution of thought: what we believe when we see or experience something informs the way we engage. The work encourages an expansion of thought beyond personal experience, helping the viewer accept whatever new thing is made real by interaction. Abstraction at some point becomes reality.

Elana Mann explores voice, sound, politics and form. She has presented her artwork in city parks, museums, galleries, and buses including: the Museum of Contemporary Art, San Diego; Commonwealth & Council, Los Angeles; Ben Maltz Gallery, Otis College of Art and Design, Los Angeles; REDCAT, Los Angeles; The Ford Foundation, New York; The Hirshhorn Museum and Sculpture Garden, Washington D.C.; A Gentil Carioca, Rio de Janeiro, Brazil; The Getty Villa, Los Angeles; LA Metro Freewaves project; Montalvo Arts Center, Saratoga, CA; and the Lu Xun Academy of Fine Arts, Shenyang, China. She is involved with numerous collaborative/collective endeavors and most recently organized Chats About Change with Robby Herbst, a series of grass-roots conversations with artists involved in creative social change. She is a recipient of awards from the California Community Foundation, the Center for Creative Innovation, the Rema Hort Mann Foundation and the Foundation for Contemporary Arts. Her projects have been covered by *Artforum, the Los Angeles Times, LA Weekly, NPR, O Globo, El País, La República*, and *X-Tra Magazine*, among others. Her writing has been published in periodicals and books such as *Afterall journal, Art 21,* and *In the Canyon, Revise the Canon.* She received her BFA with honors from Washington University in St. Louis, St. Louis, MO and her MFA from California Institute of the Arts, Valencia, CA. Mann lives in South Pasadena with her partner and son.

Meghann McCrory is an artist living in Los Angeles. She make photographs, sculpture, drawings, and performance. Originally from Albuquerque, she earned her BA in American Studies from Wellesley College, and her MFA in Art from CalArts.

Manfred Müller was born 1950 in Düsseldorf, Germany. From 1967 to 1970 he apprenticed as a technical draftsman, receiving his state license as an engineering draftsman. From 1971 to 1975 he studied visual communication at the Fachlochschule Düsseldorf and from 1976 to 1981 he attended the Kunstakademie in Düsseldorf, Germany - studying under Erwin Heerich (1922-2004). After leaving the Kunstakademie in 1981 he was awarded a Cité des Artes Scholarship, Paris, France and received grants from the city of Düsseldorf in 1983, and the German Industry Endowment of the Arts in 1985.

Jemima Wyman's most recent work focuses on patterns and masking used by marginalized groups to gain power (aka counterpower). Through this work she investigates visual resistance: specifically camouflage as a formal, social and political strategy in negotiating identity.